The Ultimate Mediterranean Diet Cookbook

2000 Days of Beginners Guide to Deliciously Healthy Eating, Cooking Recipes, and Pro Tips for Effortless Weight Management and Cultivating Daily Wellness.

Vedric Eshfard

Table of Contents

INTRODUCTION

Eating A Mediterranean Diet

The Mediterranean Diet is more than just a way of eating; it's a lifestyle that reflects the traditional dietary patterns of countries bordering the Mediterranean Sea. This diet has gained widespread recognition for its potential health benefits and has become a popular choice for those seeking a balanced and nutritious way of eating.

At its core, the Mediterranean Diet emphasizes whole, nutrient-dense foods, primarily plant-based, with a moderate intake of lean protein and healthy fats. Let's delve into the key components of this diet:

- Abundance of Fruits and Vegetables:

    The foundation of the Mediterranean Diet is a rich variety of fruits and vegetables. These provide essential vitamins, minerals, antioxidants, and fiber. The diverse array of colorful produce not only adds flavor and texture to meals but also ensures a broad spectrum of nutrients.

- Whole Grains:

    Whole grains are a staple in the Mediterranean Diet, offering complex carbohydrates, fiber, and various micronutrients. Common choices include whole wheat, barley, oats, and brown rice, contributing to sustained energy levels and promoting digestive health.

- Healthy Fats:

    Healthy fats, particularly olive oil, play a central role in this diet. Olive oil is a key source of monounsaturated fats, which are known to benefit heart health. It's used for cooking, dressing salads, and drizzling over dishes, adding a distinct Mediterranean flavor.

- Lean Proteins:

    Protein sources in the Mediterranean Diet include fish, poultry, beans, legumes, and nuts. Fish, especially fatty fish like salmon and mackerel, provides omega-3 fatty acids, contributing to heart health. Legumes and nuts offer plant-based protein, fiber, and an array of essential nutrients.

- Dairy in Moderation:

  Dairy products are consumed in moderation, with an emphasis on low-fat or fat-free options like yogurt and cheese. These provide calcium and protein without excessive saturated fats.

- Herbs and Spices:

  Herbs and spices are used generously to season dishes, reducing the need for excessive salt. This not only enhances flavor but also contributes to the antioxidant content of meals.

- Red Wine in Moderation:

  In moderation, red wine is often enjoyed with meals in the Mediterranean Diet. It provides antioxidants, particularly resveratrol, which has been associated with various health benefits.

- Regular Physical Activity:

  Beyond food choices, the Mediterranean Diet promotes an active lifestyle. Regular physical activity is considered an integral part of this approach to overall well-being.

Embracing the Mediterranean Diet involves savoring meals slowly, enjoying the social aspect of dining, and cultivating a mindful relationship with food. It's not just about what you eat but also how you eat, fostering a holistic approach to a healthy lifestyle.

The Mediterranean Pyramid

The Mediterranean Pyramid serves as a visual representation of the key principles of the Mediterranean Diet, highlighting the relative proportions of different food groups. This pyramid is a reflection of the traditional dietary patterns of countries like Greece, Italy, and Spain, where people have historically enjoyed good health and longevity.

- Base: Plant-Based Foods:

  The base of the pyramid is occupied by plant-based foods, emphasizing the importance of fruits, vegetables, whole grains, legumes, and nuts. These form the core of the diet, providing a wide array of nutrients and fiber.

- Middle Tiers: Lean Proteins and Healthy Fats:

  Moving up the pyramid, the next tiers highlight the consumption of lean proteins, such as fish, poultry, and beans, as well as healthy fats,

predominantly from olive oil. These elements contribute to satiety, support muscle health, and provide essential fatty acids.

- Top: Dairy, Eggs, Sweets, and Red Meat in Moderation:

  At the top of the pyramid are foods to be consumed in moderation. This includes dairy products, eggs, sweets, and red meat. While these can be enjoyed occasionally, the emphasis is on limiting their intake to maintain a balanced and heart-healthy diet.

- Daily Physical Activity:

  The Mediterranean Pyramid also incorporates a side panel emphasizing the importance of regular physical activity. This underscores the holistic nature of the Mediterranean lifestyle, promoting not only nutritious eating but also an active and healthy way of life.

The pyramid serves as a practical guide for individuals looking to adopt the Mediterranean Diet. It encourages a shift towards plant-based foods while allowing flexibility in incorporating other food groups in moderation. This balance aligns with the diet's reputation for promoting cardiovascular health, weight management, and overall well-being.

Health Benefits Of The Mediterranean Diet

The Mediterranean Diet is celebrated not only for its delicious and diverse flavors but also for the numerous health benefits it offers. Research has consistently shown that adhering to the principles of this diet can positively impact various aspects of health and well-being.

- Cardiovascular Health:

  One of the most well-established benefits of the Mediterranean Diet is its positive impact on cardiovascular health. The high intake of monounsaturated fats from olive oil, omega-3 fatty acids from fish, and antioxidants from fruits and vegetables collectively contribute to reducing the risk of heart disease. Studies have demonstrated that this diet can lower LDL cholesterol levels, decrease blood pressure, and improve overall heart function.

- Weight Management:

  The Mediterranean Diet is not a restrictive or fad diet, making it sustainable for the long term. Its focus on whole, nutrient-dense foods, along with the inclusion of healthy fats and lean proteins, supports satiety and helps regulate appetite. As a result, individuals following this diet may find it easier to maintain a healthy weight.

- Diabetes Prevention and Management:

  Research suggests that the Mediterranean Diet may be beneficial in preventing and managing type 2 diabetes. The emphasis on complex carbohydrates, fiber-rich foods, and healthy fats helps regulate blood sugar levels. Additionally, the anti-inflammatory and antioxidant properties of the diet may play a role in reducing insulin resistance.

- Cognitive Health:

  There is growing evidence to suggest that the Mediterranean Diet may have protective effects on cognitive function and reduce the risk of neurodegenerative diseases such as Alzheimer's. The combination of antioxidants, omega-3 fatty acids, and anti-inflammatory compounds from the diverse array of foods in this diet may contribute to brain health.

- Cancer Prevention:

  While no diet can guarantee the prevention of cancer, the Mediterranean Diet's emphasis on plant-based foods, rich in antioxidants and phytochemicals, may contribute to a lower risk of certain cancers. The

inclusion of fish, which provides omega-3 fatty acids, has also been associated with a reduced risk of certain cancers.

- Longevity and Overall Well-Being:

Populations following the Mediterranean Diet have been associated with increased longevity and improved quality of life. The combination of nutritious foods, regular physical activity, and a positive approach to meals, including the social aspect of dining, contributes to overall well-being.

- Anti-Inflammatory Effects:

Chronic inflammation is implicated in various health conditions, including cardiovascular disease, diabetes, and arthritis. The Mediterranean Diet's emphasis on foods with anti-inflammatory properties, such as olive oil, fatty fish, fruits, and vegetables, may help reduce inflammation in the body.

- Improved Gut Health:

The abundance of fiber from fruits, vegetables, and whole grains in the

Mediterranean Diet promotes a healthy gut microbiome. A balanced and diverse gut microbiota is associated with improved digestion, nutrient absorption, and overall immune function.

In conclusion, the Mediterranean Diet is more than a set of dietary guidelines; it's a holistic approach to living that combines nutritious eating, physical activity, and a positive mindset. Its health benefits extend beyond the prevention of specific diseases to encompass overall well-being and a higher quality of life. As individuals around the world continue to seek sustainable and health-promoting dietary patterns, the Mediterranean Diet stands out as a timeless and evidence-based choice.

Foods To Eat In Mediterranean Diet

The Mediterranean Diet is renowned for its health benefits and is inspired by the traditional eating patterns of countries bordering the Mediterranean Sea. This diet emphasizes fresh, whole foods that are not only delicious but also contribute to overall well-being. Here's a comprehensive look at the foods to eat in the Mediterranean Diet:

- Fruits and Vegetables:

  At the core of the Mediterranean Diet are fruits and vegetables. These are rich in vitamins, minerals, fiber, and antioxidants. Berries, tomatoes, leafy greens, artichokes, and eggplants are staples. These foods provide essential nutrients while promoting heart health and reducing the risk of chronic diseases.

- Olive Oil:

  Olive oil is a key component of the Mediterranean Diet. It is the primary source of fat and is rich in monounsaturated fats, which are heart-healthy. Use extra virgin olive oil for salads, cooking, and as a dip for bread.

- Whole Grains:

  Whole grains like brown rice, quinoa, bulgur, and whole wheat bread are important sources of fiber and complex carbohydrates in this diet. They provide sustained energy and contribute to digestive health.

- Fish and Seafood:

  Fish and seafood, particularly fatty fish like salmon, mackerel, and sardines, are high in omega-3 fatty acids. These healthy fats support brain function and reduce the risk of cardiovascular diseases.

- Lean Proteins:

  Poultry, legumes, and nuts are sources of lean protein in the Mediterranean Diet. Legumes such as chickpeas and lentils are not only rich in protein but also in fiber, making them a nutritious choice.

- Dairy:

  The Mediterranean Diet includes moderate amounts of dairy, with a focus on yogurt and cheese. These provide calcium and probiotics, promoting bone health and a healthy gut.

- Herbs and Spices:

  Herbs and spices are used generously to add flavor without relying on excessive salt. Basil, oregano, rosemary, and garlic are commonly used, contributing not just taste but also additional health benefits.

- Nuts and Seeds:

  Almonds, walnuts, and flaxseeds are common in Mediterranean cuisine. These are rich in healthy fats, protein, and various essential nutrients. They make for excellent snacks or additions to salads and dishes.

- Wine (in moderation):

  Red wine, consumed in moderation, is a characteristic aspect of the

Mediterranean Diet. It contains antioxidants and has been associated with heart health. However, excessive alcohol consumption is not recommended.

- Water:

  Staying hydrated is crucial in the Mediterranean Diet. Water is the primary beverage, promoting overall health and aiding in digestion.

- Occasional Sweets:

  While the diet does limit sweets and desserts, it doesn't eliminate them entirely. Occasional indulgences in small portions of desserts like fruit-based pastries or dark chocolate are acceptable.

- Physical Activity:

  While not a food item, physical activity is an integral part of the Mediterranean lifestyle. Regular exercise contributes to the overall health benefits associated with this diet.

In summary, the Mediterranean Diet is characterized by a diverse range of whole, unprocessed foods that provide a well-rounded and nutritionally rich approach to eating.

Suggestions For Making The Switch To A Diet Inspired By The Mediterranean

Adopting a Mediterranean-inspired diet can be a positive and rewarding lifestyle change. Here are practical suggestions to help you make the switch successfully:

- Gradual Transition:

  Start by gradually incorporating Mediterranean elements into your existing diet. Introduce more fruits, vegetables, and olive oil while reducing processed foods. This gradual approach makes the transition sustainable.

- Explore New Recipes:

  Embrace the culinary diversity of the Mediterranean region by exploring new recipes. Look for dishes from Italy, Greece, Spain, and other Mediterranean countries. Experiment with herbs, spices, and different cooking techniques to add flavor to your meals.

- Choose Whole Grains:

  Swap refined grains for whole grains. Choose whole wheat bread, brown rice, quinoa, and barley. Whole grains provide more fiber and nutrients, promoting better digestion and sustained energy.

- Prioritize Plant-Based Proteins:

Increase your intake of plant-based proteins like legumes, nuts, and seeds. Experiment with chickpea salads, lentil soups, and nut-based snacks. These alternatives are not only nutritious but also contribute to environmental sustainability.

- Include Fatty Fish:

Incorporate fatty fish like salmon, mackerel, and sardines into your diet. Aim for at least two servings of fish per week. This adds omega-3 fatty acids to your diet, supporting heart health and cognitive function.

- Snack on Nuts and Seeds:

Replace processed snacks with nuts and seeds. Almonds, walnuts, and sunflower seeds are not only satisfying but also rich in healthy fats, protein, and essential nutrients.

- Use Olive Oil Liberally:

Make extra virgin olive oil your primary cooking fat and salad dressing. Its monounsaturated fats are a hallmark of the Mediterranean Diet, providing numerous health benefits.

- Dine Mindfully:

The Mediterranean lifestyle encourages mindful eating. Sit down for meals, savor each bite, and enjoy the company of others. This approach helps regulate portion sizes and fosters a positive relationship with food.

- Moderate Dairy Consumption:

Choose moderate amounts of dairy, with a preference for yogurt and cheese. These sources of calcium contribute to bone health and provide probiotics for gut health.

- Stay Hydrated with Water:

Water is the beverage of choice in the Mediterranean Diet. Limit sugary drinks and prioritize water throughout the day. Herbal teas are also a good option.

- Limit Red Meat:

Red meat is consumed in moderation in the Mediterranean Diet. Replace some red meat meals with poultry, fish, or plant-based alternatives to reduce saturated fat intake.

- Enjoy Red Wine in Moderation:

If you consume alcohol, consider enjoying red wine in moderation. Limiting alcohol intake to one glass per day for women and two for men is associated with potential health benefits.

- Socialize and Be Active:

  Embrace the social and active aspects of the Mediterranean lifestyle. Engage in regular physical activity, whether it's walking, cycling, or other forms of exercise. Share meals with friends and family, fostering a sense of community.

- Be Mindful of Sweets:

  Sweets and desserts are enjoyed occasionally in the Mediterranean Diet. Choose small portions of high-quality desserts, such as fresh fruit or dark chocolate, to satisfy your sweet cravings.

- Educate Yourself:

  Learn about the principles of the Mediterranean Diet and the health benefits associated with it. Understanding the science behind the diet can reinforce your commitment and motivate you to make healthier choices.

In conclusion, transitioning to a Mediterranean-inspired diet involves embracing a holistic approach to food and lifestyle. By making gradual changes, exploring new recipes, and adopting mindful eating habits, you can experience the numerous health benefits associated with this flavorful and nutritious way of eating.

Chapter 1: Breakfast

Loaded Mediterranean Omelette

Prep Time: 10 Mins   Cook Time: 2 Mins   Serves: 2

Ingredients:

- 4 large eggs
- 2 tbsp fat-free milk
- 1/4 tsp baking powder (optional)
- 1/2 tsp Spanish paprika
- 1/4 tsp ground allspice
- Salt and pepper, to your liking (I used about 1/2 tsp each)
- 1 1/2 tsp Private Reserve Greek extra virgin olive oil
- 1 tzatziki sauce recipe to serve, optional
- Warm pita to serve, optional
- oppings
- 1/2 cup cherry tomatoes, halved
- 2 tbsp sliced pitted Kalamata olives
- 1/4 to 1/3 cup marinated artichoke hearts, drained and quartered
- 2 tbsp chopped fresh parsley, more for later
- 2 tbsp chopped fresh mint, more for later
- Crumbled feta cheese, to your liking, optional

Directions:

1. In a mixing bowl, add the eggs, milk, baking powder (if using), spices, salt and pepper. Quickly and vigorously whisk to combine.
2. In a 10-inch non-stick skillet, heat extra virgin olive oil until shimmering but not smoking. Be sure to tilt the skillet to coat the bottom well with oil.
3. Pour the egg mixture in and immediately stir with a heat-resistant spatula for like 5 seconds. Then push the cooked portions at the edge toward the center, tilting the pan to allow uncooked egg to fill in around the edges. When no more egg runs to the sides, continue to cook until almost set and the bottom is light golden (about 1 minute.) Remember, the omelette has more time to cook once filled and folded.
4. Remove the skillet from the heat. Spoon a good portion of the toppings onto the center third of the omelette. Use the spatula to fold. Add the remainder of the toppings on top. Sprinkle a little more fresh herbs.
5. Slice the omelette into two halves and serve hot. If you like, add a side of Greek tzatziki sauce and warm pita bread. Enjoy!

Nutritional Value (Amount per Serving):

Calories: 166; Fat: 12.59; Carb: 6.35; Protein: 7.03

Date Pine Nut Overnight Oatmeal

Prep Time: 10 Mins   Cook Time: 7 Hrs 50 Mins   Serves: 1

Ingredients:

- ½ cup old-fashioned rolled oats
- ½ cup water
- Pinch of salt
- 2 tablespoons chopped dates
- 1 tablespoon toasted pine nuts
- 1 teaspoon honey
- ¼ teaspoon ground cinnamon

Directions:

1. Combine oats, water and salt in a jar or bowl and stir. Cover and refrigerate overnight.
2. In the morning, heat the oats, if desired, or eat cold. Top with dates, pine nuts, honey and cinnamon.

Nutritional Value (Amount per Serving):

Calories: 180; Fat: 3.5; Carb: 48.22; Protein: 8.56

Mediterranean Black Olive Bread

Prep Time: 35 Mins   Cook Time: 2 Hrs   Serves: 15

Ingredients:

- 3 cups bread flour
- 2 teaspoons active dry yeast
- 2 tablespoons white sugar
- 1 teaspoon salt
- ½ cup chopped black olives
- 3 tablespoons olive oil
- 1 ¼ cups warm water (110 degrees F)
- 1 tablespoon cornmeal

Directions:

1. In a large bowl, mix together flour, yeast, sugar, salt, black olives, olive oil, and water.
2. Turn out dough onto a floured board. Knead until smooth and elastic, 5 to 10 minutes. Set aside, and let rise about 45 minutes, until it doubles in size. Punch down. Knead well again, for about 5 to 10 minutes. Let rise for about 30 minutes, until it doubles in size.
3. Round the dough on kneading board. Place upside down in a bowl lined with a lint-free, well-floured towel. Let rise until double in size.
4. While the bread is rising for the third time, put a pan of water in the bottom of the oven. Preheat oven to 500 degrees F.
5. Gently turn loaf out onto a sheet pan that has been lightly oiled and dusted with cornmeal.
6. Bake loaf at 500 degrees F for 15 minutes. Reduce heat to 375 degrees F. Bake for 30 more minutes, or until done.

Nutritional Value (Amount per Serving):

Calories: 133; Fat: 3.71; Carb: 20.94; Protein: 3.6

Mediterranean Breakfast Quinoa

Prep Time: 10 Mins   Cook Time: 15 Mins   Serves: 4

Ingredients:

- ¼ cup chopped raw almonds
- 1 teaspoon ground cinnamon
- 1 cup quinoa
- 2 cups milk
- 1 teaspoon sea salt
- 1 teaspoon vanilla extract
- 2 tablespoons honey
- 2 dried pitted dates, finely chopped
- 5 dried apricots, finely chopped

Directions:

1. Toast the almonds in a skillet over medium heat until just golden, 3 to 5 minutes; set aside.
2. Heat the cinnamon and quinoa together in a saucepan over medium heat until warmed through. Add the milk and sea salt to the saucepan and stir; bring the mixture to a boil, reduce heat to low, place a cover on the saucepan, and allow to cook at a simmer for 15 minutes. Stir the vanilla, honey, dates, apricots, and about half the almonds into the quinoa mixture. Top with the remaining almonds to serve.

Nutritional Value (Amount per Serving):

Calories: 319; Fat: 6.67; Carb: 55.82; Protein: 10.27

Hummus Tartine

Prep Time: 5 Mins   Cook Time: 5 Mins   Serves: 2

Ingredients:

- 2 slices sourdough bread or your favorite artisan-style bread, thickly sliced
- 3 tablespoons olive tapenade hummus or your hummus flavor of choice
- 6 canned artichoke hearts rinsed, drained, and split in half length-wise
- 10 sundried tomato pieces
- 2 tablespoons crumbled feta cheese

Directions:

1. With a Toaster Oven: Spread each slice of bread with hummus. Top each slice evenly with artichoke hearts, sundried tomatoes, and feta. Place in toaster oven and toast until bread is lightly crisp and topping is warm. Enjoy immediately.

2. With a Conventional Oven: Place rack in the upper third of an oven and preheat oven to 450 degrees F. Assemble tartines as directed above. Set on an ungreased baking sheet, then bake until lightly crisp, about 4 minutes, keeping a close eye on them the entire time they bake to prevent scorching.
3. With a Regular Toaster: Toast bread until golden and lightly crisp. Spread with hummus and top as directed above.

Nutritional Value (Amount per Serving):

Calories: 354; Fat: 7.36; Carb: 64.34; Protein: 17.18

Pistachio Raspberry Croissants Recipe

Prep Time: 20 Mins   Cook Time: 20 Mins   Serves: 6

Ingredients:

- 4 tablespoons (1/2 stick) unsalted butter
- 1 3/4 cups roasted, unsalted pistachios, divided
- 3 tablespoons roasted pistachio oil, such as La Tourangelle
- 1/3 cup granulated sugar
- 2 large eggs
- 1/4 teaspoon kosher salt
- 6 stale croissants, preferably 2 to 3 days old
- 1 cup simple syrup
- 1/4 cup raspberry preserves, divided
- Crushed freeze dried raspberries, for topping (optional)

Directions:

1. Place 4 tablespoons unsalted butter in a medium bowl and let sit at room temperature until softened, 30 to 45 minutes. Meanwhile, coarsely chop 1/4 cup of the roasted, unsalted pistachios. Place the remaining 1 1/2 cups pistachios in a food processor fitted with the blade attachment or a high-speed blender. Pulse until ground into very fine powder, 25 to 30 pulses.
2. Arrange a rack in the middle of the oven and heat the oven to 350°F. Line a rimmed baking sheet with parchment paper.
3. Add 3 tablespoons roasted pistachio oil and 1/3 granulated sugar to the bowl of butter. Mix with a spatula or wooden spoon until the mixture is light and just slightly grainy. Add the powdered pistachios, 2 large eggs, and 1/4 teaspoon kosher salt. Mix until smooth and creamy.
4. Slice 6 stale croissants in half horizontally with a serrated knife (like a sandwich). Be sure to slice evenly so that the halves are flat and not angled.
5. Generously brush the cut sides of the croissant halves with 1 cup simple syrup. Spread about 2 tablespoons of the pistachio cream onto each bottom croissant half. Top each portion with 2 teaspoons of the raspberry

preserves and gently smear into an even layer. Close the croissants with the tops. Spread the remaining pistachio cream over each croissant top half (about 1 tablespoon each).

6. Place the croissants on the baking sheet, spacing them evenly apart. Sprinkle with the chopped pistachios. Bake until the cream is golden-brown around the edges and the pistachios on top are toasted, 20 minutes. Immediately sprinkle with crushed freeze-dried raspberries if desired. Serve warm or at room temperature.

Nutritional Value (Amount per Serving):

Calories: 655; Fat: 33.38; Carb: 82.95; Protein: 13.46

Roasted Red Pepper Bread

Prep Time: 45 Mins   Cook Time: 20 Mins   Serves: 2

Ingredients:

- 1-1/2 cups roasted sweet red peppers, drained
- 1 package (1/4 ounce) active dry yeast
- 2 tablespoons warm water (110°F to 115°F)
- 1-1/4 cups grated Parmesan cheese, divided
- 1/3 cup warm 2% milk (110°F to 115°F)
- 2 tablespoons butter, softened
- 1-1/4 teaspoons salt
- 3-1/4 to 3-3/4 cups all-purpose flour
- 1 large egg
- 1 tablespoon water
- 1-1/2 teaspoons coarsely ground pepper

Directions:

1. Place red peppers in a food processor; cover and process until pureed. In a large bowl, dissolve yeast in warm water. Add the red peppers, 1 cup cheese, milk, butter, salt and 1-1/2 cups flour. Beat until smooth. Stir in enough remaining flour to form a firm dough.

2. Turn onto a floured surface; knead until smooth and elastic, 6-8 minutes. Place in a greased bowl, turning once to grease the top. Cover and let rise in a warm place until doubled, about 1 hour.

3. Punch dough down. Turn onto a lightly floured surface; divide dough into 6 pieces. Shape each into an 18-in. rope. Place 3 ropes on a greased baking sheet and braid; pinch ends to seal and tuck under. Repeat with remaining dough. Cover and let rise until doubled, about 1 hour.

4. In a small bowl, combine egg and water; brush over braids. Sprinkle with pepper and remaining cheese. Bake at 350° for 18-22 minutes or until golden brown.

Nutritional Value (Amount per Serving):

Calories: 756; Fat: 30.68; Carb: 89.26; Protein: 29.86

Pulled Chicken Sandwiches

Prep Time: 20 Mins   Cook Time: 4 Mins   Serves: 6

Ingredients:

- 1 medium onion, finely chopped
- 1 can (6 ounces) tomato paste
- 1/4 cup reduced-sodium chicken broth
- 2 tablespoons brown sugar
- 1 tablespoon cider vinegar
- 1 tablespoon yellow mustard
- 1 tablespoon Worcestershire sauce
- 2 garlic cloves, minced
- 2 teaspoons chili powder
- 3/4 teaspoon salt
- 1/8 teaspoon cayenne pepper
- 1-1/2 pounds boneless skinless chicken breasts
- 6 whole wheat hamburger buns, split

Directions:

1. In a small bowl, mix the first 11 ingredients. Place chicken in a 3-qt. slow cooker. Pour sauce over top.
2. Cook, covered, on low until chicken is tender, 4-5 hours. Remove chicken; cool slightly. Shred meat with 2 forks. Return to slow cooker; heat through. Serve on buns.

Nutritional Value (Amount per Serving):

Calories: 500; Fat: 17.93; Carb: 45.14; Protein: 38.63

Chapter 2: Salads and Sides Dishes

Greek Kale Salad With Creamy Tahini Dressing

Prep Time: 20 Mins   Cook Time: 5 Mins   Serves: 4

Ingredients:

- ale Salad
- 1 medium bunch of curly green kale (about 8 ounces)
- Fine sea salt
- 1 can (15 ounces) chickpeas, rinsed and drained, or 1 1/2 cups cooked chickpeas
- 1/2 cup thinly sliced Kalamata olives and/or roughly chopped pepper rings
- 1/3 cup oil-packed sun-dried tomatoes, rinsed and drained
- 1/3 cup finely grated Parmesan (optional)
- 1/3 cup sunflower seeds
- 1/4 teaspoon extra-virgin olive oil
- reamy Tahini Dressing
- ¼ cup tahini
- 3 tablespoons lemon juice (from 1 to 1 1/2 lemons)
- 1 tablespoon extra-virgin olive oil
- 1 medium clove garlic, pressed or minced
- 1/2 teaspoon Dijon mustard
- 1/4 teaspoon fine sea salt
- 2 tablespoons water
- Freshly ground black pepper, to taste

Directions:

1. To prepare the salad: Place the chopped kale in a large serving bowl. Sprinkle it lightly with salt and massage it with your hands by scrunching up large handfuls at a time until it's darker and more fragrant (this makes the kale more tasty and easier to eat). Add the chickpeas, olives and/or pepper rings, sun-dried tomatoes, and Parmesan (if using). Set aside.
2. To toast the sunflower seeds, combine the seeds with the olive oil and a few dashes of salt in a small skillet over medium heat. Cook, stirring often, until the seeds are fragrant and turning lightly golden at the edges, about 5 minutes. Pour the toasted seeds into the salad bowl.
3. To prepare the salad dressing: In a small liquid measuring cup or bowl, combine the tahini, olive oil, lemon juice, garlic, mustard, and salt. Whisk until blended. Add the water and whisk until blended. Season generously with freshly black pepper, to taste.
4. Pour the dressing into the salad (you might not need quite all of it, but I did). Toss until the salad is evenly coated with dressing. Serve immediately. This salad keeps well in the refrigerator, covered, for up to 3 days.

Nutritional Value (Amount per Serving):

Calories: 846; Fat: 60.88; Carb: 38.94; Protein: 43.21

Baked Spaghetti Squash

Prep Time: 10 Mins   Cook Time: 50 Mins   Serves: 4

Ingredients:

- 1 tablespoon olive oil
- 1 spaghetti squash, halved and seeded

Directions:

1. Preheat the oven to 350 degrees F. Lightly grease a baking sheet with olive oil.
2. Place spaghetti squash, cut-side down, on the baking sheet.
3. Bake in the preheated oven until skin can easily be pierced with a fork and spaghetti squash is tender, 40 to 60 minutes, depending on size of spaghetti squash.
4. Remove from oven and allow to rest until cool enough to handle. Scrape out flesh with a fork and discard skins.

Nutritional Value (Amount per Serving):

Calories: 38; Fat: 3.52; Carb: 1.74; Protein: 0.16

Toasted Sesame Hummus

Prep Time: 15 Mins   Cook Time: 3 Mins   Serves: 1 3/4

Ingredients:

- 1/4 cup tahini
- 1/4 cup lemon juice (from 1 1/2 to 2 lemons)
- 2 tablespoons extra-virgin olive oil
- 1 medium clove garlic
- 1/2 teaspoon fine sea salt
- 1 1/2 teaspoons toasted sesame oil, divided, more to taste
- 1 can (15 ounces) chickpeas, rinsed and drained, or 1 1/2 cups cooked chickpeas
- 2 to 4 tablespoons water, as needed
- 1 teaspoon raw sesame seeds (I used a mix of white and black)
- Flaky sea salt, for garnish (optional)
- Suggested accompaniments: Toasted pita bread, carrot or bell pepper or celery sticks, crackers, etc.

Directions:

1. In a food processor or high-powered blender (i.e., Vitamix or Blendtec), combine the tahini, lemon juice, olive oil, garlic, salt, and 1/2 teaspoon of the sesame oil. Process for about 1 1/2 minutes, pausing to scrape down the

sides and bottom as necessary, until the mixture is smooth and creamy.

2. Add half of the chickpeas to the food processor and process for 1 minute. Scrape down the bowl, then add the remaining chickpeas and process until the hummus is thick and smooth, 1 to 2 more minutes.

3. While running the food processor, drizzle in 2 to 4 tablespoons of water, until it reaches your desired consistency and level of creaminess. Taste and season with additional salt (I added 1/4 teaspoon) and toasted sesame oil, if you want more pronounced sesame flavor (about 1/2 teaspoon). Set aside.

4. Toast the sesame seeds in a small skillet over medium heat, shimmying the skillet frequently, until they're starting to turn golden, about 2 to 4 minutes. Pour them into a bowl to prevent them from burning.

5. Scrape the hummus into a small serving bowl. Lightly drizzle 1 teaspoon sesame oil over the top. Sprinkle generously with sesame seeds and a light sprinkle of flaky sea salt (if using). Serve with accompaniments of your choice. Leftover hummus keeps well, chilled, for 4 to 5 days.

Nutritional Value (Amount per Serving):

Calories: 247; Fat: 14.87; Carb: 22.98; Protein: 7.92

Summer Millet Salad

Prep Time: 25 Mins   Cook Time: 20 Mins   Serves: 8

Ingredients:

- 1 cup millet
- 2¼ cups water or vegetable broth
- 4 scallions, chopped
- 1 pint cherry tomatoes, quartered
- 1¼ cups cubed Havarti cheese
- 1 cup parsley leaves
- 1 lemon, zested and juiced
- ⅓cup olive oil
- Kosher salt and freshly ground black pepper

Directions:

1. In a medium saucepan, combine the millet with the water or broth. Bring to a simmer over medium heat. Cover the pot and reduce the heat to low.

2. Simmer until the liquid is absorbed and the millet is fluffy, 12 to 15 minutes. Drain the millet in a strainer and cool to room temperature.

3. In a large bowl, toss the cooled millet with the scallions, tomatoes, cheese, parsley and lemon zest.

4. Pour the lemon juice and olive oil over the mixture and toss to coat. Season with salt and pepper to taste. Reserve in an airtight container in the refrigerator until ready to serve (it will keep for up to five days).

Nutritional Value (Amount per Serving):

Calories: 395; Fat: 24.83; Carb: 24.02; Protein: 18.81

Mediterranean Chickpea Salad I

Prep Time: 15 Mins   Cook Time: 3 Hrs   Serves: 4

Ingredients:

- 1 (15 ounce) can garbanzo beans (chickpeas), drained and rinsed
- ½ cup oil-packed sun-dried tomatoes, drained and cut into strips
- 1 cup crumbled feta cheese
- 1 red onion, chopped
- 2 cloves garlic, minced
- 1 tablespoon chopped fresh cilantro
- 2 tablespoons olive oil
- 2 tablespoons lemon juice
- salt to taste

Directions:

1. In a bowl, mix the garbanzo beans, sun-dried tomatoes, feta cheese, onion, garlic, and cilantro.
2. In a separate bowl, whisk together the olive oil, lemon juice, and salt, and pour over the salad. Refrigerate at least 3 hours before serving.

Nutritional Value (Amount per Serving):

Calories: 294; Fat: 18.41; Carb: 23.45; Protein: 11.39

Roasted Cauliflower And Farro Salad With Feta And Avocado

Prep Time: 15 Mins   Cook Time: 30 Mins   Serves: 4

Ingredients:

- oasted Cauliflower
- 1 large head cauliflower (about 2 pounds), cut into bite-sized florets
- 2 tablespoons extra-virgin olive oil
- 1/4 teaspoon red pepper flakes (scale back or omit if sensitive to spice)
- 1/4 teaspoon fine sea salt
- arlicky Farro
- 1 cup uncooked farro, rinsed
- 2 teaspoons extra-virgin olive oil
- 2 cloves garlic, pressed or minced
- 1/4 teaspoon fine sea salt
- verything Else
- 1/3 cup pitted Kalamata olives, rinsed, half sliced into small rounds and the rest halved lengthwise

- 1/4 cup oil-packed sun-dried tomatoes, rinsed and roughly chopped
- 1/2 cup crumbled feta (about 2 ounces)
- 1 tablespoon lemon juice (about 1/2 lemon), plus more for serving
- Freshly ground black pepper, to taste
- 1 avocado, sliced into thin strips
- 4+ handfuls leafy greens (spring greens, spinach, arugula or baby kale are all good choices)

Directions:

1. To roast the cauliflower: Preheat the oven to 425 degrees Fahrenheit. Toss the cauliflower florets with the olive oil, red pepper flakes and salt, and arrange it in an even layer across the pan. Roast for 25 to 35 minutes, tossing halfway, until the cauliflower is tender and deeply golden on the edges.

2. To cook the farro: In a medium saucepan, combine the rinsed farro with at least three cups water (enough water to cover the farro by a couple of inches). Bring the water to a boil, then reduce the heat to a gentle simmer, and cook until the farro is tender to the bite but still pleasantly chewy. (Pearled farro will take around 15 minutes; unprocessed farro will take 25 to 40 minutes.) Drain off the excess water and mix in the olive oil, garlic and salt. Set aside.

3. In a large serving bowl, toss together the roasted cauliflower, cooked farro, olives, sun-dried tomatoes, feta and lemon juice. Taste and season with additional salt and pepper if necessary.

4. Divide the avocado and greens between four dinner plates. Top with a generous amount of the cauliflower and farro salad. Finish the plates with an extra squeeze of lemon juice or drizzle of olive oil, if desired. Serve promptly.

Nutritional Value (Amount per Serving):

Calories: 529; Fat: 33.44; Carb: 34.11; Protein: 27.89

Mediterranean-Style Homemade Salsa Recipe

Prep Time: 10 Mins   Cook Time: 0 Min   Serves: 4

Ingredients:

- 12 oz cherry tomatoes, cut into quarters
- 1 to 2 shallots, finely chopped
- 1 garlic clove, minced
- 1/2 cup chopped fresh parsley
- 1/2 cup chopped fresh mint
- 6 to 7 pitted kalamata olives, chopped (optional)

- 1 jalapeno pepper, finely chopped (optional if you want to add spice)
- Kosher salt and pepper
- 1/2 tsp to 1 tsp sumac
- 2 to 3 tsp lemon juice
- Extra virgin olive oil (I used Early Harvest Greek extra virgin olive oil)

Directions:

1. Place quartered cherry tomatoes, chopped shallots, minced garlic, chopped fresh herbs, chopped kalamata olives (if using), and chopped jalapeno (if using) in a mixing bowl.
2. Season with kosher shalt, pepper, and sumac (start with a heaping 1/2 tsp sumac, add more late if needed). Toss gently.
3. Add lemon juice and a generous drizzle of quality extra virgin olive oil (I used Early Harvest EVOO). Toss to combine. Set aside for a few minutes to let the flavors marry.
4. Serve with pita chips or chips of your choice. Enjoy!

Nutritional Value (Amount per Serving):

Calories: 114; Fat: 3.2; Carb: 16.53; Protein: 6.54

Tortellini Salad With Marinated Artichokes And Feta

Prep Time: 15-20 Mins   Cook Time: 2-7 Mins   Serves: 6

Ingredients:

- 1 small clove garlic
- 1 small shallot
- 2 medium lemons
- 2 tablespoons olive oil
- 1/2 teaspoon Dijon mustard
- 1/2 teaspoon kosher salt
- 1/4 teaspoon freshly ground black pepper
- 1 small red or orange bell pepper
- 1 small head radicchio
- 1 (12-ounce) jar marinated artichoke hearts
- 1/2 cup pitted Kalamata olives
- 1 (20-ounce) package fresh cheese tortellini, or 2 (12-ounce) packages frozen cheese tortellini
- 4 ounces feta cheese

Directions:

1. Bring a large pot of salted water to a boil. Meanwhile, prepare the following, adding them to a large bowl as you complete them: Mince 1 small garlic clove, thinly slice 1 small shallot (about 1/4 cup), and squeeze 2

medium lemons until you have 3 tablespoons juice.

2. Add 2 tablespoons olive oil, 1/2 teaspoon Dijon mustard, 1/2 teaspoon kosher salt, and 1/4 teaspoon black pepper, and whisk to combine.

3. Prepare the following, adding them to the vinaigrette as you complete them: Thinly slice 1 small orange bell pepper, then cut the slices in half. Halve, core, and thinly slice 1 small head radicchio (about 1 1/4 cups). Drain and halve 1 jar marinated artichoke hearts and 1/2 cup pitted Kalamata olives. Stir to combine.

4. Add the cheese tortellini to the boiling water and cook according to package instructions until al dente, 2 to 7 minutes. Drain well and add the warm tortellini to the salad. Crumble 4 ounces feta cheese into the salad (about 1 cup). Toss to combine. Taste and season with more kosher salt and black pepper as needed.

Nutritional Value (Amount per Serving):

Calories: 327; Fat: 16; Carb: 33.93; Protein: 14.17

Greek Orzo Salad Recipe

Prep Time: 15 Mins   Cook Time: 10 Mins   Serves: 6 To 8

Ingredients:

- 8 ounces orzo pasta (1 ¼ cup dry)
- 1 cup canned chickpeas, drained and rinsed
- 1/2 lemon, juice and zest (about 2 tablespoons juice)
- ¼ cup minced shallot or red onion
- 1/2 English cucumber (2 cups diced, or substitute a peeled standard cucumber)
- 2 roasted red peppers from a jar or ½ fresh red bell pepper (½ cup diced)
- ⅓cup chopped dill, plus more for garnish
- ⅓cup chopped mint
- 2 tablespoons white wine vinegar
- 3 tablespoons extra-virgin olive oil
- ½ teaspoon Dijon mustard
- 1 teaspoon dried oregano
- ½ cup feta cheese crumbles
- ⅓cup Kalamata olives, halved
- Black pepper

Directions:

1. Prepare the orzo according to the package instructions. Taste the orzo a few minutes before completion to ensure it's 'al dente' (chewy, but with a little firmness in the center). When it's done, drain it and then rinse it under cold water until it comes to room temperature.

2. Place the chickpeas in a bowl with the lemon zest, lemon juice, and 1/4 teaspoon kosher salt.

3. Mince the red onion, then place it in a bowl with water (this helps to remove the sharp onion taste). Dice the cucumber. Dice the roasted red

pepper. Chop the herbs.

4. Stir together the orzo, chickpeas and bowl of lemon juice, red onion, cucumber, red pepper, dill, mint, white wine vinegar, olive oil, Dijon mustard, oregano, feta crumbles, black olives, and several grinds of black pepper. Taste and if necessary, season with more kosher salt.

Nutritional Value (Amount per Serving):

Calories: 165; Fat: 7.1; Carb: 19.06; Protein: 7.02

Quinoa, Asparagus, and Feta Salad

Prep Time: 15 Mins   Cook Time: 20 Mins   Serves: 6

Ingredients:

- alad:
- 1 ½ cups water
- ¾ cup quinoa
- ¼ teaspoon salt
- 1 bunch fresh asparagus, trimmed and cut into 1 1/2-inch pieces
- 4 ounces crumbled feta cheese
- ⅓ cup toasted slivered almonds
- 2 green onions, thinly sliced, or to taste
- 2 tablespoons chopped fresh parsley
- 1 teaspoon chopped fresh thyme
- 1 lemon, zested
- ressing:
- ¼ cup lemon juice
- 2 tablespoons olive oil
- 1 tablespoon honey
- 1 clove garlic, minced
- 1 ½ teaspoons Dijon mustard
- freshly ground black pepper to taste

Directions:

1. Pour water into a saucepan and bring to a boil; add quinoa and salt, stir, cover saucepan with a lid, and reduce heat to low. Simmer mixture until quinoa is tender, 10 to 15 minutes. Remove saucepan from heat, let quinoa rest for 5 minutes, and transfer quinoa to a bowl to cool.

2. Bring a large pot of lightly salted water to a boil. Add asparagus and cook uncovered until tender but still crisp, 2 to 3 minutes; drain in a colander and immediately immerse asparagus in ice water for several minutes until cold to stop the cooking process. Drain.

3. Stir asparagus, feta cheese, almonds, green onions, parsley, thyme, and lemon zest into quinoa.

4. Whisk lemon juice, olive oil, honey, garlic, Dijon mustard, and black pepper together in a bowl until dressing is smooth. Pour dressing over quinoa mixture and stir gently to combine.

Nutritional Value (Amount per Serving):

Calories: 347; Fat: 20.89; Carb: 20.35; Protein: 19.57

Chapter 3: Grain, Pasta and Rice

Mediterranean Pasta with Greens

Prep Time: 15 Mins   Cook Time: 20 Mins   Serves: 8

Ingredients:

- 1 (16 ounce) package dry fusilli pasta
- 1 bunch Swiss chard, stems removed
- 2 tablespoons olive oil
- ½ cup oil-packed sun-dried tomatoes, chopped
- ½ cup pitted, chopped kalamata olives
- ½ cup pitted, chopped green olives
- 1 clove garlic, minced
- ¼ cup fresh grated Parmesan cheese

Directions:

1. Bring a large pot of lightly salted water to a boil. Stir in pasta, cook for 10 to 12 minutes, until al dente, and drain.
2. Place chard in a microwave safe bowl. Fill bowl about 1/2 full with water. Cook on High in the microwave 5 minutes, until limp; drain.
3. Heat the oil in a skillet over medium heat. Stir in the sun-dried tomatoes, kalamata olives, green olives, and garlic. Mix in the chard. Cook and stir until tender. Toss with pasta and sprinkle with Parmesan cheese to serve.

Nutritional Value (Amount per Serving):

Calories: 81; Fat: 7.04; Carb: 4.04; Protein: 1.54

Instant Pot Chicken Risotto

Prep Time: 10 Mins   Cook Time: 30 Mins   Serves: 6

Ingredients:

- 1 teaspoon dried oregano
- 1 teaspoon dried thyme
- 1 teaspoon paprika
- ½ teaspoon salt
- ¼ teaspoon freshly ground black pepper
- 1 pound boneless, skinless chicken thighs, chopped
- 3 tablespoons butter, divided
- 1 tablespoon olive oil
- ½ cup diced onion
- 3 cloves garlic, minced
- 2 cups Arborio rice
- ½ cup dry white wine

- 4 ½ cups chicken stock
- ½ cup freshly grated Parmesan cheese
- salt and ground black pepper to taste
- 1 sprig fresh parsley, chopped

Directions:

1. Turn on a multi-functional pressure cooker, and select Saute function on normal setting according to manufacturer's instructions.
2. Mix oregano, thyme, paprika, salt, and pepper in a small bowl. Season chicken with spice blend.
3. Heat 1 tablespoon butter and olive oil in the pressure cooker until butter is melted. Quickly brown chicken on all sides, about 3 minutes. Remove chicken. Add onion and cook until translucent, about 2 minutes. Add garlic and cook until fragrant, about 30 seconds. Remove onion and garlic from the pot.
4. Melt a second tablespoon of butter in the pot, add rice, and stir constantly until fully coated and toasted, about 3 minutes. Pour in wine and scrape up any browned bits from the bottom with a wooden spoon. Cook until wine is absorbed and alcohol cooks off, about 2 minutes. Add chicken stock, chicken, and onion mixture to the pot; mix until well combined. Turn off Saute function.
5. Close and lock the lid. Select high pressure according to manufacturer's instructions, and set timer for 5 minutes. Allow 10 to 15 minutes for pressure to build.
6. Release pressure carefully using the quick-release method according to manufacturer's instructions, about 5 minutes. Unlock and remove the lid. Stir Parmesan cheese and remaining tablespoon of butter into the risotto. Season with salt and pepper, garnish with chopped parsley, and serve.

Nutritional Value (Amount per Serving):

Calories: 492; Fat: 27.78; Carb: 46.99; Protein: 25.29

Lasagna Alfredo

Prep Time: 30 Mins   Cook Time: 1 Hr 15 Mins   Serves: 8

Ingredients:

- 1 (16 ounce) package lasagna noodles
- 1 (10 ounce) package frozen chopped spinach
- 3 cooked, boneless chicken breast halves, diced
- 2 (16 ounce) jars Alfredo-style pasta sauce, divided
- 2 pints ricotta cheese
- 4 cups shredded mozzarella cheese

- salt and ground black pepper to taste

Directions:

1. Preheat the oven to 350 degrees F.
2. Bring a large pot of lightly salted water to a boil. Add lasagna noodles and cook until tender yet firm to the bite, 8 to 10 minutes; drain.
3. Place frozen spinach and 1/2 cup water in a 2-quart nonstick saucepan; bring to a boil. Reduce heat to medium-high, cover, and cook, stirring occasionally, until spinach is tender, 6 to 7 minutes. Drain and squeeze out any excess water.
4. Stir together chicken and 1 jar Alfredo sauce in a medium bowl until well combined.
5. Mix together ricotta and spinach in a second medium bowl until well combined.
6. Arrange a single layer of lasagna noodles in a 9x13-inch baking dish, edges overlapping. Pour chicken-Alfredo mixture over noodles and spread evenly. Sprinkle with 1 cup mozzarella. Cover with another layer of noodles. Spread spinach mixture evenly over noodles. Pour 1/2 of the remaining jar of Alfredo sauce over spinach mixture and spread evenly. Sprinkle with 1 cup mozzarella. Lay on a final noodle layer and top with remaining 1/2 jar Alfredo sauce and 2 cups mozzarella. Season with salt and pepper.
7. Bake in the preheated oven until the top is brown and bubbly, 50 to 60 minutes.

Nutritional Value (Amount per Serving):

Calories: 228; Fat: 8.28; Carb: 12.29; Protein: 26.73

Mediterranean Brown Rice Salad

Prep Time: 15 Mins   Cook Time: 45 Mins   Serves: 6

Ingredients:

- 1 ½ cups uncooked brown rice
- 3 cups water
- 1 red bell pepper, thinly sliced
- 1 cup frozen green peas, thawed
- ½ cup raisins
- ¼ sweet onion (such as Vidalia), chopped
- ¼ cup chopped Kalamata olives
- ½ cup vegetable oil
- ¼ cup balsamic vinegar
- 1 ¼ teaspoons Dijon mustard
- salt and ground black pepper to taste
- ¼ cup feta cheese

Directions:

1. Bring brown rice and water to a boil in a saucepan over high heat. Reduce heat to medium-low; cover and simmer until rice is tender and the liquid is

absorbed, 45 to 50 minutes.

2. Combine red bell pepper, peas, raisins, onion, and olives in a bowl.
3. Whisk vegetable oil, vinegar, and mustard together in a separate bowl for the balsamic dressing.
4. Stir brown rice and balsamic dressing into vegetable mixture. Season with salt and black pepper.
5. Top brown rice and vegetables with feta cheese before serving.

Nutritional Value (Amount per Serving):

Calories: 252; Fat: 22.83; Carb: 9.14; Protein: 4.18

Carrot, Tomato, and Spinach Quinoa Pilaf

Prep Time: 10 Mins   Cook Time: 25 Mins   Serves: 5

Ingredients:

- 2 teaspoons olive oil
- ½ onion, chopped
- 1 cup quinoa
- 2 cups water
- 2 tablespoons vegetarian chicken-flavored bouillon granules
- 1 teaspoon ground black pepper
- 1 teaspoon thyme
- 1 carrot, chopped
- 1 tomato, chopped
- 1 cup baby spinach

Directions:

1. Heat olive oil in a saucepan over medium heat. Cook and stir onion in hot oil until translucent, about 5 minutes. Lower heat, stir in quinoa, and toast, stirring constantly, for 2 minutes. Stir in water, bouillon granules, pepper, and thyme; increase heat to high and bring to a boil. Cover, reduce heat to low, and simmer for 5 minutes.
2. Stir in carrots. Cover and simmer until all water is absorbed, about 10 minutes. Turn off heat, add tomatoes and spinach, and stir until spinach is wilted and tomatoes have released all their moisture, about 2 minutes.

Nutritional Value (Amount per Serving):

Calories: 302; Fat: 9.67; Carb: 45.59; Protein: 8.92

Make-Ahead Mediterranean Egg Casserole

Prep Time: 10 Mins   Cook Time: 35-40 Mins   Serves: 8 To 10

Ingredients:

- 1 teaspoon olive oil, plus more for the pan
- 1/2 small red onion

- 2 cloves garlic
- 1 (14-ounce) can water-packed artichokes
- 1 cup grape or cherry tomatoes (about 5 ounces)
- 1 tablespoon fresh oregano leaves
- 4 ounces feta cheese, crumbled (about 1 cup)
- 1/2 ounce Parmesan cheese, finely grated (about 1/4 cup)
- 1 1/4 teaspoons kosher salt, divided
- 6 ounces baby spinach (about 6 cups)
- 12 Eggland's Best large eggs
- 2 cups whole or 2% milk
- 1/4 teaspoon freshly ground black pepper

Directions:

1. Arrange a rack in the middle of the oven and heat the oven to 375°F. Coat a 9x13-inch baking dish with olive oil.
2. Prepare the vegetables and cheeses: Thinly slice 1/2 small red onion. Finely chop 2 garlic cloves. Drain and coarsely chop 1 can artichokes. Halve 1 cup grape or cherry tomatoes, or quarter if large. Finely chop 1 tablespoon fresh oregano leaves. Crumble 4 ounces 1 cup feta cheese (about 1 cup). Finely grate 1/2 ounces Parmesan cheese (about 1/4 cup).
3. Heat 1 teaspoon olive oil in a large skillet over medium-high heat until shimmering. Add the red onion and 1/2 teaspoon of the kosher salt, and cook until soft, 2 to 3 minutes. Add the garlic and artichokes and cook until the garlic is fragrant, about 1 minute. Add 6 ounces spinach (about 6 cups) and cook until just wilted, about 2 minutes.
4. Transfer the vegetables to the prepared baking dish and arrange in an even layer. Sprinkle the tomatoes and feta cheese evenly over the vegetables.
5. Whisk the Parmesan, oregano, 12 Eggland's Best large eggs, 2 cups whole or 2% milk, 1/4 teaspoon black pepper, and remaining 3/4 teaspoon kosher salt together in a large bowl until combined. Pour the egg mixture over the vegetables.
6. Bake until puffed, set, and an instant-read thermometer inserted into the center reads 160°F, about 30 minutes. Let the casserole cool for 10 minutes before serving.

Nutritional Value (Amount per Serving):

Calories: 208; Fat: 13.22; Carb: 11.93; Protein: 10.91

Wild Rice Bowl With Red Lentil-Coconut Curry And Spinach

Prep Time: 45 Mins   Cook Time: 25 Mins   Serves: 4

Ingredients:

- 1 cup wild rice
- 2 tablespoons ghee (or butter, or coconut oil)
- 1 medium yellow onion, diced
- 3 cloves garlic, minced
- 1 teaspoon minced ginger
- 1 cup red lentils
- 1 tablespoon red curry paste
- 1 tablespoon tomato paste
- 1 tablespoon curry powder
- 1 teaspoon coriander
- 1 teaspoon turmeric
- 1/2 teaspoon cayenne powder (optional)
- 3 1/2 cups vegetable broth
- 2 cups baby spinach leaves, tightly packed
- 1 (15.5-ounce) can coconut milk
- 1/2 cup Greek yogurt
- 1/4 cup cilantro leaves (lightly packed), to garnish

Directions:

1. Prepare the wild rice according to the package instructions, or follow these simple steps. Most wild rice takes about 45 minutes to become tender; you can also make it a few days ahead so it's ready when you need it.
2. While the rice is cooking, heat the ghee in a large saucepan with tall sides over medium-high heat. Add the diced onion and cook until lightly golden and soft. Add in the minced garlic and ginger, and sauté for another 2 to 3 minutes. Add in the red lentils, red curry paste, tomato paste, and spices, and cook until fragrant. Pour in the broth and bring to a boil.
3. Once the lentils and broth reach a boil, reduce to a simmer, cover, and cook for 15 to 20 minutes, or until the lentils are soft. Before serving, fold in the fresh spinach leaves, and pour in the coconut milk. At this point, taste the curry and adjust the seasoning according to your liking; add more salt or cayenne, if needed.
4. To serve, divide the wild rice equally into 4 bowls. Top each bowl with the curry, a dollop of yogurt, and fresh cilantro leaves. Serve immediately.

Nutritional Value (Amount per Serving):

Calories: 634; Fat: 23.23; Carb: 85.94; Protein: 27.28

Shrimp Pasta with Roasted Red Peppers and Artichokes

Prep Time: 10 Mins   Cook Time: 25 Mins   Serves: 8

Ingredients:

- 12 ounces farfalle pasta , bow tie or other pasta
- 1 ½ pounds fresh or frozen medium shrimp in shells
- ¼ cup butter
- 3 cloves garlic , minced
- 1 12- ounce jar roasted red bell peppers , drained and chopped
- 1 cup canned artichoke hearts in water or brine , quartered
- ½ cup dry white wine
- 3 tablespoons drained capers
- ½ cup whipping cream
- 1 teaspoon finely shredded lemon peel
- 2 tablespoons lemon juice
- ¾ cup crumbled feta cheese , 3 ounces
- 2 ounces toasted pine nuts
- ¼ cup snipped fresh basil

Directions:

1. In a Dutch oven cook pasta according to package directions; drain. Return pasta to hot Dutch oven; cover and keep warm. Meanwhile, thaw shrimp, if frozen. Peel and devein shrimp, leaving tails intact if desired. Rinse shrimp; pat dry with paper towels.
2. In a 12-inch skillet heat butter over medium-high heat until melted. Add garlic; cook and stir for 1 minute. Add shrimp; cook and stir for 2 minutes. Add roasted re peppers, artichokes, wine, and capers.
3. Bring to boiling; reduce heat. Simmer, uncovered, about 2 minutes or until shrimp are opaque, stirring occasionally. Stir in whipping cream, lemon peel, and lemon juice. Return to boiling; reduce heat. Boil gently, uncovered, for 1 minute more.
4. Pour shrimp mixture over cooked pasta; toss gently to combine. Garnish with feta cheese, pine nuts and basil.

Nutritional Value (Amount per Serving):

Calories: 343; Fat: 19.36; Carb: 36.45; Protein: 8.66

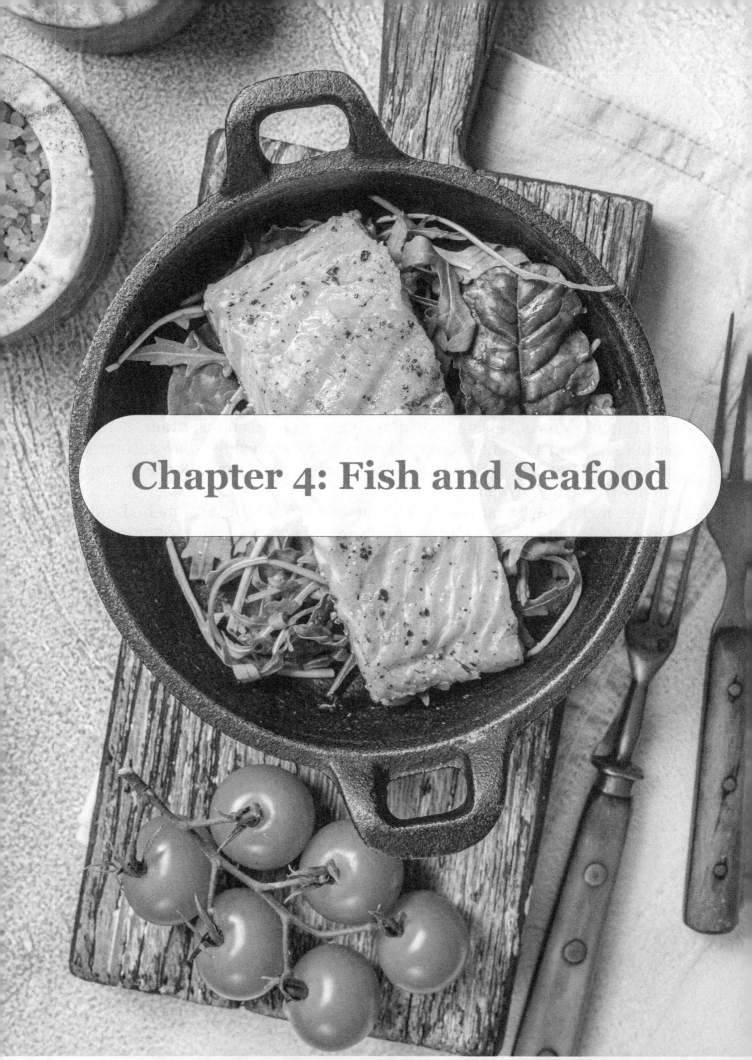

Chapter 4: Fish and Seafood

Roasted Cod Nicoise

Prep Time: 15 Mins   Cook Time: 35 Mins   Serves: 4

Ingredients:

- cooking spray
- 1 ½ pounds small new red potatoes, cut into 1-inch chunks
- 2 tablespoons olive oil, divided
- ¼ teaspoon salt
- 8 ounces thin French-style green beans, trimmed
- 1 ½ teaspoons coarse-ground Dijon mustard
- ⅛ teaspoon salt
- ⅛ teaspoon ground black pepper
- 4 (6 ounce) cod fillets
- 3 tablespoons prepared black olive tapenade
- 6 lemon wedges, or to taste
- 1 cup grape tomatoes, halved
- 2 tablespoons chopped fresh parsley

Directions:

1. Preheat the oven to 400 degrees F. Line an extra-large rimmed baking sheet with parchment paper. Coat parchment with cooking spray.
2. Toss potatoes in a bowl with 1 1/2 tablespoon oil and 1/4 teaspoon salt. Transfer to the prepared baking sheet and roast for 20 minutes.
3. Toss green beans in bowl with remaining 1/2 tablespoon oil, mustard, remaining 1/8 teaspoon salt, and pepper. Push potatoes to one side of the baking sheet. Lay beans and fish separately on the other side. Spread 3/4 tablespoon tapenade on each fillet.
4. Bake until cod is no longer translucent and flakes easily with a fork, 12 to 15 minutes. If vegetables need more time, transfer cod to a plate and cover with foil to keep warm. Roast vegetables 5 to 10 more minutes.
5. Serve with lemon wedges, tomatoes, and parsley.

Nutritional Value (Amount per Serving):

Calories: 407; Fat: 13.97; Carb: 44.43; Protein: 28.07

Ginger Salmon with Cucumber Lime Sauce

Prep Time: 30 Mins   Cook Time: 10 Mins   Serves: 10

Ingredients:

- 1 tablespoon grated lime zest
- 1/4 cup lime juice

- 2 tablespoons olive oil
- 2 tablespoons rice vinegar or white wine vinegar
- 4 teaspoons sugar
- 1/2 teaspoon salt
- 1/2 teaspoon ground coriander
- 1/2 teaspoon freshly ground pepper
- 1/3 cup chopped fresh cilantro
- 1 tablespoon finely chopped onion
- 2 teaspoons minced fresh gingerroot
- 2 garlic cloves, minced
- 2 medium cucumbers, peeled, seeded and chopped
- almon:
- 1/3 cup minced fresh gingerroot
- 1 tablespoon lime juice
- 1 tablespoon olive oil
- 1/2 teaspoon salt
- 1/2 teaspoon freshly ground pepper
- 10 salmon fillets (6 ounces each)

Directions:

1. Place the first 13 ingredients in a blender. Cover and process until pureed.
2. In a small bowl, mix ginger, lime juice, oil, salt and pepper. Rub over flesh side of salmon fillets.
3. Lightly oil the grill rack. Place salmon on rack, skin side down. Grill, covered, over medium-high heat 10-12 minutes or until fish just begins to flake easily with a fork. Serve with sauce.

Nutritional Value (Amount per Serving):

Calories: 799; Fat: 41.57; Carb: 4.62; Protein: 95.32

Sheet-Pan Salmon with Sweet Potatoes Broccoli

Prep Time: 30 Mins   Cook Time: 15 Mins   Serves: 4

Ingredients:

- 3 tablespoons low-fat mayonnaise
- 1 teaspoon chili powder
- 2 medium sweet potatoes, peeled and cut into 1-inch cubes
- 4 teaspoons olive oil, divided
- ½ teaspoon salt, divided
- ¼ teaspoon ground pepper, divided
- 4 cups broccoli florets (8 oz.; 1 medium crown)
- 1 ¼ pounds salmon fillet, cut into 4 portions

- 2 limes, 1 zested and juiced, 1 cut into wedges for serving
- ¼ cup crumbled feta or cotija cheese
- ½ cup chopped fresh cilantro

Directions:

1. Preheat oven to 425 degrees F. Line a large rimmed baking sheet with foil and coat with cooking spray.
2. Combine mayonnaise and chili powder in a small bowl. Set aside.
3. Toss sweet potatoes with 2 tsp. oil, 1/4 tsp. salt, and 1/8 tsp. pepper in a medium bowl.
4. Spread on the prepared baking sheet. Roast for 15 minutes.
5. Meanwhile, toss broccoli with the remaining 2 tsp. oil, 1/4 tsp. salt, and 1/8 tsp. pepper in the same bowl.
6. Remove the baking sheet from oven. Stir the sweet potatoes and move them to the sides of the pan. Arrange salmon in the center of the pan and spread the broccoli on either side, among the sweet potatoes.
7. Spread 2 Tbsp. of the mayonnaise mixture over the salmon.
8. Bake until the sweet potatoes are tender and the salmon flakes easily with a fork, about 15 minutes.
9. Meanwhile, add lime zest and lime juice to the remaining 1 Tbsp. mayonnaise; mix well.
10. Divide the salmon among 4 plates and top with cheese and cilantro.
11. Divide the sweet potatoes and broccoli among the plates and drizzle with the lime-mayonnaise sauce. Serve with lime wedges and any remaining sauce.

Nutritional Value (Amount per Serving):

Calories: 379; Fat: 18.93; Carb: 18.95; Protein: 33.24

Honey Balsamic Glazed Salmon

Prep Time: 5 Mins   Cook Time: 10 Mins   Serves: 4

Ingredients:

- 4 salmon fillets 5 ounce
- 1 teaspoon olive oil
- 2 cloves garlic minced
- 1 tablespoon honey
- 1/3 cup balsamic vinegar
- 4 teaspoons Dijon mustard
- salt and pepper to taste
- 1 tablespoon chopped fresh oregano for garnish

Directions:

1. Preheat oven to 400 degrees. Line a baking sheet with aluminum foil and spray with cooking spray.
2. In a medium saucepan cook the garlic until tender in the olive oil about 2-3 minutes. Add honey, balsamic vinegar, dijon mustard, and salt and pepper

to taste. Simmer for about 3 minutes until it slightly starts to thicken. Remove from heat.

3. Place the salmon fillets on the aluminum lined baking sheet. Brush the salmon with the balsamic glaze but reserve half for brushing on a the end.

4. Bake for about 6-10 minutes until flesh flakes easily with a fork. Brush them remaining glaze.

Nutritional Value (Amount per Serving):

Calories: 693; Fat: 31.24; Carb: 10.07; Protein: 86.69

Sheet-Pan Roasted Salmon Vegetables

Prep Time: 35 Mins   Cook Time: 20 Mins   Serves: 4

Ingredients:

- 1 pound fingerling potatoes, halved lengthwise
- 2 tablespoons olive oil
- 5 garlic cloves, coarsely chopped
- ½ teaspoon sea salt
- ½ teaspoon freshly ground black pepper
- 4 5 to 6-ounce fresh or frozen skinless salmon fillets
- 2 medium red, yellow and/or orange sweet peppers, cut into rings
- 2 cups cherry tomatoes
- 1 ½ cups chopped fresh parsley (1 bunch)
- ¼ cup pitted kalamata olives, halved
- ¼ cup finely snipped fresh oregano or 1 Tbsp. dried oregano, crushed
- 1 lemon

Directions:

1. Preheat oven to 425 degrees F. Place potatoes in a large bowl. Drizzle with 1 Tbsp. of the oil and sprinkle with garlic and 1/8 tsp. of the salt and black pepper; toss to coat. Transfer to a 15x10-inch baking pan; cover with foil. Roast 30 minutes.

2. Meanwhile, thaw salmon, if frozen. Combine, in the same bowl, sweet peppers, tomatoes, parsley, olives, oregano and 1/8 tsp. of the salt and black pepper. Drizzle with remaining 1 Tbsp. oil; toss to coat.

3. Rinse salmon; pat dry. Sprinkle with remaining 1/4 tsp. salt and black pepper. Spoon sweet pepper mixture over potatoes and top with salmon. Roast, uncovered, 10 minutes more or just until salmon flakes.

4. Remove zest from lemon. Squeeze juice from lemon over salmon and vegetables. Sprinkle with zest.

Nutritional Value (Amount per Serving):

Calories: 552; Fat: 26.39; Carb: 35.32; Protein: 43.57

Grilled Citrus Salmon with Pineapple Salsa

Prep Time: 15 Mins   Cook Time: 15 Mins   Serves: 4

Ingredients:

- 1/4 cup orange juice
- 1/4 cup lemon juice
- 1/4 cup lime juice
- 1/4 cup orange marmalade
- 2 garlic cloves minced
- 3 Tablespoons Soy Sauce
- 1/4 cup brown sugar
- 1 Tablespoon Cornstarch
- 1 Tablespoon Water
- Reynolds Wrap Non-Stick Aluminum Foil
- 2 pounds salmon filet
- Recipe for Pineapple Salsa
- Optional Garnish:
- Sliced orange lemon, and lime

Directions:

1. In a medium sized saucepan whisk together orange juice, lemon juice, lime juice, orange marmalade, garlic, soy sauce, and brown sugar. In a small bowl combine cornstarch and water and whisk into the sauce. Heat to medium high heat and let simmer until it starts to thicken. Remove from heat.
2. Heat grill to medium high heat. On a sheet of Reynolds Wrap Aluminum Foil place the salmon on top. Fold up the edges of the aluminum foil. Spread on half of the marinade. Place the foil on the grill and let the salmon cook for 10-12 minutes or until salmon is opaque and cooked throughout. Spread remaining marinade on top and serve.

Nutritional Value (Amount per Serving):

Calories: 499; Fat: 19.86; Carb: 28.68; Protein: 49.98

Spanish Cod In Tomato Sauce

Prep Time: 10 Mins   Cook Time: 20 Mins   Serves: 6

Ingredients:

- 3 tablespoons olive oil
- 2 pounds cod file cut in 6 pieces or if you prefer cut in smaller bite size chunks(like the one from Trader Joe's)
- 2 tablespoons all-purpose flour
- 1 medium onion diced
- 3-4 garlic cloves diced
- 1 medium size green bell pepper
- 1 medium size red bell pepper
- 14 ounces tomato puree 1 can

- 1-2 bay leaves
- 1/2 teaspoon smoked or regular paprika
- salt and pepper to taste
- 1/2 teaspoon granulated sugar

Directions:

1. Place the flour on a plate and toss the pieces of cod in it. Set aside.
2. Heat a nonstick frying pan on medium-high heat and add the extra virgin olive oil.
3. After 2 minutes or when the olive oil is hot, add the cod pieces and fry them 2-3 minutes on each side. Transfer them into a separate dish and set them aside.
4. Using the same pan, add the diced onions and garlic and mix them with the oil. Scrap up anything that was left over from frying the cod and mix it with the onions.
5. Add the green and red bell pepper and cook together about 5 minutes. Add salt and pepper to your taste and the smoked or regular paprika.
6. Add the can of tomatoes, sugar and the Bay leaves and mix together until well combined.
7. Reduce the heat to low and simmer the sauce until the peppers are cooked, about 5 minutes.
8. Return the cod to the pan and allow the sauce and fish to simmer together for 2 more minutes. Taste the sauce for salt and pepper.
9. Serve directly from the pan.

Nutritional Value (Amount per Serving):

Calories: 727; Fat: 13.63; Carb: 150.04; Protein: 2.45

Pepper and Salsa Cod

Prep Time: 10 Mins   Cook Time: 20 Mins   Serves: 4

Ingredients:

- 2 cod or haddock fillets (6 ounces each)
- 1 teaspoon olive oil
- 1/4 teaspoon salt
- Dash pepper
- 1/3 cup orange juice
- 1/4 cup salsa
- 1/3 cup julienned green pepper
- 1/3 cup julienned sweet red pepper
- Hot cooked rice

Directions:

1. Preheat oven to 350°F. Brush both sides of fillets with oil; place in a greased 11x7-in. baking dish. Sprinkle with salt and pepper. Pour orange juice over fish; top with salsa and peppers.
2. Bake, covered, until fish just begins to flake easily with a fork, 17-20 minutes. Serve with rice.

Nutritional Value (Amount per Serving):

Calories: 216; Fat: 3.47; Carb: 12.05; Protein: 33.07

Mediterranean Baked White Fish

Prep Time: 10 Mins   Cook Time: 15 Mins   Serves: 6

Ingredients:

- 1 ½ lb white fish fillet such as cod or halibut, (1 to 1 ½ in thickness)
- Kosher salt and ground black pepper
- Extra virgin olive oil
- Juice of ½ lemon more for later
- 8 ounces cherry tomatoes, halved
- 3 ounces pitted olives, halved (I used a combination of kalamata olives and green olives)
- 3 tablespoons minced red onion
- 4 to 5 garlic cloves, minced
- 1 tablespoon fresh thyme leaves
- 2 teaspoons dried oregano

Directions:

1. Heat the oven to 425 degrees F.
2. Pat the fish dry and season with salt and pepper on both sides. Brush a 9 ½ x 13-inch baking dish with a little extra virgin olive oil and put the fish in it. Squeeze ½ lemon juice all over the top of the fish.
3. In a medium mixing bowl, combine the tomatoes, olives, onions, garlic and spices. Add a very small pinch of salt and ground pepper. Add a generous drizzle (about 3 tablespoons extra virgin olive oil) toss to combine.
4. Pour the tomato and olive mixture over the fish.
5. Bake in the heated oven for 15 to 20 minutes (this will depend on the thickness of your fish).
6. Remove from the heat and serve.

Nutritional Value (Amount per Serving):

Calories: 142; Fat: 3.49; Carb: 29.56; Protein: 1.77

Shrimp And Polenta

Prep Time: 15 Mins   Cook Time: 1 Hr   Serves: 4

Ingredients:

- or The Polenta:
- ¾ cup fine-grind cornmeal

- ¼ cup medium-grind cornmeal
- 4 cups cold water
- 1 teaspoon fine salt
- 2 tablespoons unsalted butter or ghee
- or The Shrimp:
- 3 tablespoons extra-virgin olive oil
- 2 cloves garlic, finely chopped
- ½ to 1 teaspoon red pepper flakes
- ½ cup dry white wine (such as Soave or Vermentino)
- ½ cup water
- ½ teaspoon fine salt
- 1 pound large wild shrimp, 31-40 per pound, peeled and deveined
- 2 tablespoons finely chopped flat-leaf parsley
- Juice of ½ lemon
- 1 tablespoon unsalted butter or ghee

Directions:

1. Make the polenta. Preheat the oven to 350°F. In a heavy-bottomed Dutch oven or high-sided saucepan, whisk together the cornmeal, water, and salt. Cover the pot and place in the hot oven. Bake the polenta for 50 minutes, then remove it from the oven and stir vigorously with a whisk to break up the mass of polenta and give it a smooth creamy consistency. Taste for doneness (careful—it's hot!). If it's still a little chalky, cover and return it to the oven for 10 minutes. Stir in 2 tablespoons butter or ghee and whisk until well combined. Turn off the oven, cover the pot and return the polenta to the oven to keep warm.

2. Make the shrimp. Place the 3 tablespoons of olive oil, the garlic, and the red pepper flakes in a large, wide skillet and set over medium-low to low heat. Cook, stirring often, until the garlic is softened and fragrant but not browned. Raise the heat to medium-high and stir in the wine and water. Sprinkle in the salt. Bring to a simmer and cook until reduced by about half.

3. Add the shrimp. Lower the heat to medium and add the shrimp to the pan in a single layer. Cook for 2 minutes, until pink on the bottom. Turn and cook on the other side for about 1 minute. Sprinkle 1 tablespoon of parsley over the shrimp and add the lemon juice. Stir or swirl gently while the shrimp finish cooking. After another minute, add 1 tablespoon butter or ghee to the pan and swirl to incorporate it into the sauce. Remove from the heat.

4. Remove the polenta from the oven. Place 4 shallow bowls into the oven to warm briefly—1 to 2 minutes, just to take the chill off. Spoon a bed of polenta into each warmed bowl and top with shrimp. Spoon a little of the pan sauce from the shrimp over each serving. Sprinkle with parsley and serve.

Nutritional Value (Amount per Serving):

Calories: 668; Fat: 12.61; Carb: 121.57; Protein: 20.46

Chapter 5: Pizza, Wraps, and Sandwiches

Grilled Peanut Butter Apple Sandwiches

Prep Time: 10 Mins   Cook Time: 5 Mins   Serves: 4

Ingredients:

- ½ teaspoon ground cinnamon
- ½ teaspoon white sugar
- 8 tablespoons creamy peanut butter
- 8 slices whole wheat bread
- 1 large Gala apple, peeled, cored, and thinly sliced
- ¼ cup unsalted butter

Directions:

1. Mix cinnamon and sugar together in a small bowl.
2. Spread 1 tablespoon peanut butter onto each bread slice.
3. Arrange apple slices on 1/2 of the bread slices. Sprinkle cinnamon-sugar mixture evenly over apples. Sandwich remaining bread slices over apples with peanut butter facing down.
4. Melt butter in a very large skillet over medium heat. Working in batches if necessary, cook sandwiches in the hot skillet until golden brown, 1 to 2 minutes per side.

Nutritional Value (Amount per Serving):

Calories: 650; Fat: 32.23; Carb: 76.15; Protein: 23.17

Bakery-Style Pizza

Prep Time: 25 Mins   Cook Time: 1 Hr 55 Mins   Serves: 12

Ingredients:

- ough:
- 1 ¼ cups warm water
- 1 teaspoon active dry yeast
- 3 cups bread flour
- 1 ½ teaspoons fine salt
- ¼ cup olive oil, divided
- auce:
- 1 (28 ounce) can plain crushed tomatoes
- 1 (14 ounce) can pizza sauce
- heese:
- 8 ounces low-moisture whole-milk mozzarella, very thinly sliced
- ¼ cup grated Pecorino Romano cheese

Directions:

1. Make dough: Combine warm water and yeast in a small bowl. Let stand until yeast softens and forms a creamy foam, about 5 minutes. Combine flour and salt together in the bowl of a stand mixer fitted with a dough hook attachment. Pour in yeast mixture. Knead dough until smooth, about 7 minutes.
2. Grease a large bowl lightly with olive oil. Form dough into a tight ball and place in the prepared bowl, turning to coat. Cover the bowl loosely with

plastic wrap. Let rise until doubled in volume, about 30 minutes.

3. Meanwhile, make sauce: Mix crushed tomatoes and pizza sauce together in a medium bowl until well combined.

4. Grease a heavy-gauge rimmed 12x17-inch baking sheet generously with some olive oil.

5. Press dough into the prepared baking sheet. Prick dough all over with a fork. Arrange mozzarella cheese slices over dough; cover with 1 cup sauce. Sprinkle Pecorino Romano cheese on top. Drizzle remaining olive oil over pizza. Let rise in a warm area until puffy, about 1 hour.

6. Preheat the oven to 450 degrees F.

7. Bake pizza on the center rack in the preheated oven until the edges are very dark brown, but the top is not burnt, 15 to 20 minutes. Cool in the pan for 5 minutes before slicing into squares.

Nutritional Value (Amount per Serving):

Calories: 246; Fat: 10.81; Carb: 27.34; Protein: 9.47

Simple Greek Avocado Sandwich

Prep Time: 10 Mins   Cook Time: 0 Min   Serves: 1

Ingredients:

- 2 slices soft whole wheat bread
- 1/2 avocado
- 1 tablespoon basil pesto
- roasted red bell pepper (jarred is fine)
- cucumber, sliced into thin rounds
- thinly sliced red onion
- 6 pitted kalamata olives, thinly sliced
- handful spring mix
- balsamic reduction or regular balsamic vinegar

Directions:

1. Pit and peel the avocado half and mash it with a fork. Use a butter knife to spread avocado on one slice of bread. Spread a layer of pesto on the other slice of bread.

2. Top the avocado bread with a single layer of roasted red bell pepper. Then add a layer of cucumber slices, red onion, olives and spring mix. Use a spoon to sprinkle some balsamic reduction over the lettuce. Place the pesto slice on top, pesto side down.

Nutritional Value (Amount per Serving):

Calories: 911; Fat: 51.42; Carb: 94.35; Protein: 31.86

Baked Falafel

Prep Time: 20 Mins   Cook Time: 20 Mins   Serves: 2

Ingredients:

- ¼ cup chopped onion
- 1 (15 ounce) can garbanzo beans, rinsed and drained
- ¼ cup chopped fresh parsley
- 3 cloves garlic, minced
- 1 teaspoon ground cumin
- ¼ teaspoon ground coriander
- ¼ teaspoon salt
- ¼ teaspoon baking soda
- 1 tablespoon all-purpose flour
- 1 egg, beaten
- 2 teaspoons olive oil

Directions:

1. Wrap onion in cheese cloth and squeeze out as much moisture as possible. Set aside. Place garbanzo beans, parsley, garlic, cumin, coriander, salt, and baking soda in a food processor. Process until the mixture is coarsely pureed. Mix garbanzo bean mixture and onion together in a bowl. Stir in the flour and egg. Shape mixture into four large patties and let stand for 15 minutes.
2. Preheat an oven to 400 degrees F.
3. Heat olive oil in a large, oven-safe skillet over medium-high heat. Place the patties in the skillet; cook until golden brown, about 3 minutes on each side.
4. Transfer skillet to the preheated oven and bake until heated through, about 10 minutes.

Nutritional Value (Amount per Serving):

Calories: 314; Fat: 13.19; Carb: 35.76; Protein: 14.66

Pizza Boats

Prep Time: 10 Mins   Cook Time: 12 Mins   Serves: 4

Ingredients:

- 2(8-inch) hoagie rolls
- 1 tablespoon olive oil
- 2 teaspoons Italian seasoning
- 1 cup pizza sauce

- 2 cups shredded mozzarella cheese
- 8 slices pepperoni, halved
- 8 grape tomatoes, halved
- 1 tsp crushed red pepper flakes (optional)
- salt to taste

Directions:

1. Preheat the oven to 425 degrees F. Place a piece of aluminum foil on a baking sheet; set aside.
2. Slice each hoagie roll in half lengthwise to form two rolls, and using your fingertips, hollow out some of the bread inside, forming a well. Lightly brush each roll with olive oil, and sprinkle with Italian seasoning.
3. Fill and spread each roll with 1/4 cup pizza sauce and then top with 1/2 cup mozzarella cheese. Layer pepperoni and grape tomatoes on top of the cheese, sprinkle with red pepper flakes, and season to taste with salt. Place rolls on the prepared baking sheet.
4. Bake in the preheated oven until the cheese is turning golden brown and starting to bubble, 12 to 14 minutes. Serve warm.

Nutritional Value (Amount per Serving):

Calories: 238; Fat: 6.67; Carb: 21.63; Protein: 22.63

Italian Chicken Wrap

Prep Time: 10 Mins   Cook Time: 0 Min   Serves: 1

Ingredients:

- 1 extra large tortilla , flatbread or lavash bread
- 2 tablespoons DeLallo Roasted Pepper Bruschetta
- 5-6 slices cooked chicken breast , about 3 ounces
- Handful of arugula or spinach
- 2 slices provolone cheese
- 3-4 thin slices of tomato
- 2 tablespoons DeLallo Artichoke Bruschetta
- 10 kalamata or black olives , sliced
- Sliced red onion
- DeLallo Balsamic glaze

Directions:

1. Lay the tortilla or flatbread on a flat surface. Starting on the edge closest to you, layer a stripe of red pepper bruschetta about ½ inch inside the outer edge. Place the chicken slightly overlapping the bruschetta, then add a strip of arugula, then the provolone cheese and the tomato. Top with the artichoke bruschetta then the olives and sliced red onion and drizzle lightly

with the balsamic glaze.

2. Starting from the edge closest to you, fold the portion of the tortilla with the red pepper and chicken into itself, and fold the outer edges of the sides inward, then continue to tightly roll and wrap the sandwich. Slice the wrap in half and server, or cut the halves into even portions to serve as pinwheels. Make the day before or refrigerate for 2-3 days.

Nutritional Value (Amount per Serving):

Calories: 2303; Fat: 97.47; Carb: 50.62; Protein: 299.87

Pizza Bombs

Prep Time: 15 Mins   Cook Time: 15 Mins   Serves: 8

Ingredients:

- 1 (16 ounce) can refrigerated biscuits
- 1/2 cup pizza sauce, or as needed
- 1/2 cup shredded mozzarella cheese, or as needed
- 1/2 cup pepperoni, or as needed
- 1/4 cup melted butter
- 1/2 tablespoons grated Parmesan cheese, or to taste
- 1 teaspoon Italian seasoning

Directions:

1. Preheat the oven to 375 degrees F. Line a baking sheet with parchment paper.
2. Pop open the biscuit can and divide into 8 biscuits. Flatten each biscuit with your thumb into a 1/8-inch thick circle.
3. Spread the center of each circle with about 1 tablespoon pizza sauce, leaving a 1/4-inch edge open. Sprinkle each circle with about 1 tablespoon mozzarella cheese, and about 1 tablespoon pepperoni.
4. Pull up the edges of each circle to form a ball, and seal completely. Roll them in your hands to ensure the dough is sealed, then set each ball on the baking sheet seal-side-down.
5. Brush each ball with melted butter. Sprinkle with Parmesan cheese and Italian seasoning.
6. Bake in the preheated oven until golden brown, about 15 minutes. Serve with additional warmed pizza sauce for dipping.

Nutritional Value (Amount per Serving):

Calories: 87; Fat: 6.56; Carb: 4.23; Protein: 3.05

Caramelized Mushroom Flatbread Pizza

Prep Time: 20-30 Mins   Cook Time: 35-45 Mins   Serves: 4 To 6

Ingredients:

- 1 pound pizza dough, at room temperature at least 1 hour
- 1 pound cremini mushrooms
- 4 cloves garlic
- 2 teaspoons fresh thyme leaves
- 1 cup shredded part-skim mozzarella cheese, divided
- 4 tablespoons olive oil, divided
- 1/2 teaspoon kosher salt, divided
- 1/4 teaspoon freshly ground black pepper, divided
- All-purpose flour, for dusting
- Finely ground cornmeal, for dusting
- 2 tablespoons grated Parmesan cheese, divided
- 2 tablespoons chopped fresh parsley leaves, divided

Directions:

1. If using refrigerated pizza dough, make sure it sits out at room temperature for about an hour before beginning. Arrange a rack in the bottom third of the oven. Place a heavy, rimmed baking sheet upside down on the rack, and heat the oven to 450°F. Meanwhile, cut the mushrooms into 1/4-inch thick slices. Mince the 4 garlic cloves. Strip the leaves from the thyme sprigs until you have 2 teaspoons, then add to the garlic. Shred the mozzarella cheese until you get 1 cup.

2. Heat 1 tablespoon olive oil in a large skillet over medium heat until shimmering. Add half the mushrooms in a single layer and cook undisturbed until browned on the bottom, about 5 minutes. Season with 1/4 teaspoon of the salt and 1/8 teaspoon of the pepper and cook, stirring once or twice, until the mushrooms are browned all over and tender, 2 to 3 minutes more. Transfer to a medium bowl.

3. Add 1 tablespoon olive oil to the pan and repeat with the remaining mushrooms, salt, and pepper. About a minute before the mushrooms are ready, add the garlic and thyme and sauté until fragrant, about 1 minute. Transfer to the bowl of mushrooms and stir to combine. Set aside to cool while you prepare the dough.

4. Divide the pizza dough into 2 pieces. If the dough is sticky, dust with a little bit of all-purpose flour. Sprinkle a 12-inch piece of parchment paper with cornmeal and place one of the pieces of dough on it. Use the heel of your hand to press the dough flat. Using your hands or a rolling pin, work from the middle out to shape the dough into a 10-inch round. The dough will stick to the parchment; if it starts to shrink back, wait a few minutes to

let it relax and continue shaping.

5. Brush the dough with 1 tablespoon olive oil, then scatter half of the mushroom mixture onto the dough, leaving a 1/2-inch border. Sprinkle with half of the mozzarella cheese. Carefully remove the preheated baking sheet from the oven and use the parchment paper to slide the flatbread directly onto the back of the baking sheet.

6. Bake until the edges are golden-brown and crisp and the cheese is melted,10 to 12 minutes. Meanwhile, grate enough Parmesan cheese until you have 2 tablespoons. Chop until you have 2 tablespoons chopped parsley leaves.

7. Remove the baking sheet from the oven and carefully transfer the flatbread to a clean cutting board. Save the parchment paper to make a second flatbread and return the baking sheet to the oven. Top the baked flatbread with half of the Parmesan and half of the parsley. Cool for 2 minutes, then slice and serve. Repeat with the remaining dough, olive oil, and toppings.

Nutritional Value (Amount per Serving):

Calories: 885; Fat: 35.24; Carb: 117.11; Protein: 36.38

Open Faced Egg Sandwiches with Arugula Salad

Prep Time: 15 Mins   Cook Time: 5 Mins   Serves: 2

Ingredients:

- 1 clove garlic, minced
- ¼ cup mayonnaise
- 4 3/4-inch thick slices of crusty bread
- 2 cups arugula
- 2 teaspoons olive oil
- ½ teaspoon fresh lemon juice
- 1 pinch salt
- 1 pinch freshly ground black pepper
- cooking spray
- 4 eggs

Directions:

1. Mix garlic and mayonnaise together in a small bowl. Spread mayonnaise on 1 side of the bread slices. Mix arugula with olive oil, lemon juice, salt, and black pepper in a bowl until coated; divide arugula in fourths, placing each portion atop mayonnaise side of a bread slice.

2. Spray a skillet with cooking spray, place over medium-high heat, and crack eggs into skillet, one at a time. Cook on one side only until whites are firm and yolks are slightly runny, 2 to 3 minutes. Season eggs with salt and black pepper. Gently place an egg on each open-face sandwich.

Nutritional Value (Amount per Serving):

Calories: 1002; Fat: 67.6; Carb: 29.3; Protein: 65.05

Greek-Inspired Burgers with Herb-Feta Sauce

Prep Time: 25 Mins   Cook Time: 12 Mins   Serves: 4

Ingredients:

- 1 cup nonfat plain Greek yogurt
- ¼ cup crumbled feta cheese
- 3 tablespoons chopped fresh oregano, divided
- ¼ teaspoon lemon zest
- 2 teaspoons lemon juice
- ¾ teaspoon salt, divided
- 1 small red onion
- 1 pound ground lamb or ground beef
- ½ teaspoon ground pepper
- 2 whole-wheat pitas, halved, split and warmed
- 1 cup sliced cucumber
- 1 plum tomato, sliced

Directions:

1. Preheat grill to medium-high or preheat broiler to high.
2. Mix yogurt, feta, 1 tablespoon oregano, lemon zest, lemon juice and 1/4 teaspoon salt in a small bowl.
3. Cut 1/4-inch-thick slices of onion to make 1/4 cup. Finely chop more onion to make 1/4 cup. (Reserve any remaining onion for another use.) Mix the chopped onion and meat in a large bowl with the remaining 2 tablespoons oregano and 1/2 teaspoon each salt and pepper. Form into 4 oval patties, about 4 inches by 3 inches.
4. Grill or broil the burgers, turning once, until an instant-read thermometer registers 160 degrees F, 4 to 6 minutes per side. Serve in pita halves, with the sauce, onion slices, cucumber and tomato.

Nutritional Value (Amount per Serving):

Calories: 372; Fat: 18.4; Carb: 15.62; Protein: 35.22

Chapter 6: Poultry and Turkey

Mediterranean Chicken And Farro Bake

Prep Time: 15 Mins   Cook Time: 1 Hr   Serves: 4

Ingredients:

- or The Farro:
- 1 cup uncooked farro
- 3 cups vegetable or chicken broth
- or The Chicken:
- 4 small boneless skinless chicken breasts (about 2 lbs)
- 1/2 tsp kosher salt
- 1/2 tsp freshly cracked black pepper
- 1/2 tsp garlic powder
- 2 tbsp balsamic vinegar
- 2 tbsp olive oil
- or The Tomato Topping:
- 1 pint cherry tomatoes
- 1 cup canned white beans, drained (such as canellini)
- 3 cloves garlic, minced
- 1/4 tsp salt
- 1/4 tsp pepper
- 2 tbsp balsamic
- 1 tsp chopped fresh basil
- 4 oz grated mozzarella cheese

Directions:

1. Cook the farro. In a saucepan, bring the farro and broth to a boil. Cover, turn the heat to low
2. and simmer for 30 minutes. Drain any excess liquid. Spread prepared farro in a lightly greased 9x13 baking dish.
3. Marinate the chicken. Place chicken breasts in a bowl or zip-top bag with salt, pepper, garlic, balsamic vinegar and oil. Stir to evenly coat and place in the refrigerator to marinate while the farro cooks.
4. Heat oven to 350°F.
5. Place tomatoes and white beans in a large bowl. Add garlic, salt, pepper, balsamic and basil. Stir to combine.
6. Heat a large skillet over medium heat. Sear chicken for 3-4 minutes per side. Place on top of farro in the baking dish.
7. Spread tomato mixture around the chicken. Top evenly with mozzarella. Cover and bake 20 minutes, then uncover and bake until chicken is cooked through, 10-20 minutes, depending on the thickness of the chicken. The chicken should reach an internal temperature of 165°F when it is done.
8. Drizzle with additional balsamic vinegar and sprinkle with fresh basil (optional).

Nutritional Value (Amount per Serving):

Calories: 730; Fat: 20.84; Carb: 51.08; Protein: 84.7

Juicy Grilled Whole Chicken, Mediterranean-Style

Prep Time: 20 Mins   Cook Time: 1 Hr   Serves: 6

Ingredients:

- arinade
- ⅓cup extra virgin olive oil
- Juice and zest of 2 lemons
- 1 tablespoon dry oregano
- 1 tablespoon fresh thyme
- 1 teaspoon coriander
- 1 teaspoon paprika
- ½ teaspoon cumin
- ½ teaspoon black pepper
- ½ teaspoon cayenne pepper more if you like spicy
- 12 garlic cloves peeled and minced
- or Chicken
- 3 ½ lb Whole Chicken

Directions:

1. Spatchcock (butterfly) the chicken (or ask your butcher to do it). Place the chicken on a cutting board with its backbone facing you. Using a pair of sturdy kitchen shears like this one (affiliate link) cut out the backbone by cutting along both sides of the spine, and remove it. Push down on the breasts to flatten the chicken. Flip the bird over and remove the wing tips.
2. Season the chicken. Pat chicken dry and season with salt all over, lift the skin and apply salt underneath.
3. Mix the marinade. In a small bowl, mix together the marinade ingredients (olive oil, lemon juice, oregano, thyme, spices, and minced garlic cloves).
4. Apply the marinade to the chicken. Place the chicken in a large dish (with sides so that the marinade does not spill). Apply the majority of the marinade underneath the chicken skins (this will ensure best flavor), and be sure to rub some of the marinade on the back side of the chicken as well. Keep the chicken flat with skin side up. Marinate in the fridge for 2 to 4 hours.
5. Grill. Preheat an outdoor grill over medium-high (400 degrees F) and make sure to lightly oil the grates. Place the chicken over indirect heat (this means, the burner or burners directly below the chicken should be turned off, while the outer burners surrounding it should remain on. Watch the video to see how Adam does this). Cover and cook for 45 minutes to 1 hour or until the chicken's internal temp reaches 165 degrees F. Check every few minutes, and if the chicken gains some color on one part, rotate as needed.
6. Rest. Remove the chicken from the heat and set aside to rest for 10 minutes before slicing through to serve.

Nutritional Value (Amount per Serving):

Calories: 788; Fat: 28.88; Carb: 56.4; Protein: 75.9

Italian-Flavored Turkey Meatloaf

Prep Time: 10 Mins   Cook Time: 55 Mins   Serves: 4

Ingredients:

- cooking spray
- 1 pound lean ground turkey

- ½ cup Italian-style seasoned bread crumbs
- ½ cup grated Parmesan cheese
- 1 large egg
- 1 tablespoon Italian seasoning
- 1 teaspoon chopped garlic
- 1 teaspoon ground black pepper
- 1 teaspoon salt
- 1 (8 ounce) can tomato sauce
- ½ cup shredded mozzarella cheese

Directions:

1. Preheat the oven to 375 degrees F. Spray a 9-inch square baking dish with cooking spray.
2. Mix together turkey, bread crumbs, Parmesan cheese, egg, Italian seasoning, garlic, pepper, and salt in a medium bowl until well combined. Form mixture into a loaf and place in the prepared baking dish.
3. Bake in the preheated oven for 45 minutes. Pour tomato sauce over the meatloaf and bake for 5 more minutes.
4. Sprinkle mozzarella cheese over top and bake until cheese is melted and an instant-read thermometer inserted into the center of the meatloaf reads at least 160 degrees F, about 5 more minutes.

Nutritional Value (Amount per Serving):

Calories: 355; Fat: 14.47; Carb: 21.38; Protein: 32.56

Mediterranean Chicken with Eggplant

Prep Time: 50 Mins   Cook Time: 30 Mins   Serves: 5

Ingredients:

- 3 eggplants, peeled and cut lengthwise into 1/2 inch thick slices
- 3 tablespoons olive oil
- 6 skinless, boneless chicken breast halves - diced
- 1 onion, diced
- 2 tablespoons tomato paste
- ½ cup water
- 2 teaspoons dried oregano
- salt and pepper to taste

Directions:

1. Place eggplant strips in a big pot of lightly salted water and soak for 30 minutes (this will improve the taste; they will leave a brown color in the pot).
2. Remove eggplant from pot and brush lightly with olive oil. Saute or grill until lightly browned and place in a 9x13 inch baking dish. Set aside.
3. Saute diced chicken and onion in a large skillet over medium heat. Stir in tomato paste and water, cover skillet, reduce heat to low and simmer for 10 minutes.
4. Preheat oven to 400 degrees F.

5. Pour chicken/tomato mixture over eggplant. Season with oregano, salt and pepper and cover with aluminum foil. Bake in the preheated oven for 20 minutes.

Nutritional Value (Amount per Serving):

Calories: 512; Fat: 16.2; Carb: 23.73; Protein: 67.68

Saucy Mediterranean Chicken with Rice

Prep Time: 15 Mins   Cook Time: 15 Mins   Serves: 4

Ingredients:

- 3/4 cup water
- 3 tablespoons tomato paste
- 2 tablespoons lemon juice
- 3/4 teaspoon salt
- 1 teaspoon chili powder
- 1/2 teaspoon garlic powder
- 1/2 teaspoon ground ginger
- 1/4 teaspoon ground fennel seed
- 1/4 teaspoon ground turmeric
- 1 teaspoon ground coriander, optional
- 3 tablespoons olive oil
- 1 medium onion, chopped
- 1 pound boneless skinless chicken breasts, cut into 1-inch cubes
- 3 cups hot cooked rice
- Minced fresh parsley, optional

Directions:

1. In a small bowl, mix the water, tomato paste, lemon juice, salt, chili powder, garlic powder, ginger, fennel, turmeric and, if desired, coriander until smooth.
2. In a large skillet, heat oil over medium-high heat. Add onions; cook and stir until tender. Stir in chicken; brown 3-4 minutes. Pour water mixture into pan.
3. Bring to a boil. Reduce heat; simmer, uncovered, until chicken is no longer pink, 8-10 minutes. Serve with rice. If desired, top with parsley.

Nutritional Value (Amount per Serving):

Calories: 538; Fat: 31.9; Carb: 51.28; Protein: 38.84

Healthy Greek Chicken With Tzatziki Sauce

Prep Time: 40 Mins   Cook Time: 20 Mins   Serves: 4

Ingredients:

- reek Seasoning:
- 1 tsp salt
- 2 tsp garlic powder
- 1 tsp onion powder
- 2 tsp dried basil
- 2 tsp dried Greek oregano

- 2 tsp paprika
- 1 tsp freshly ground black pepper
- 1 tsp dried rosemary, minced
- 1 tsp dried dill
- 1 tsp dried marjoram
- 1/2 tsp ground thyme
- 1/2 tsp ground nutmeg
- reek Chicken:
- Juice of 2 large lemons
- 2 tbsp red wine vinegar
- 2 tbsp olive oil
- 4 tbsp Greek seasoning
- 2 large boneless, skinless chicken breast
- zatziki Sauce:
- 1/4 medium cucumber
- 1 cup plain Greek yogurt
- 2 cloves garlic, minced
- 2 tbsp chopped fresh dill
- Juice of 1/2 lemon
- 1/8 tsp salt
- Pinch black pepper

Directions:

1. To make Greek seasoning, mix all spices together. It will make about 1/2 cup. Set aside for later.
2. For the chicken, butterfly boneless, skinless chicken breasts into 2 pieces of even thickness each. Rub Greek seasoning evenly over chicken. Place in a shallow dish or large plastic bag with lemon juice, red wine vinegar and olive oil. Let marinate for at least 30 minutes.
3. While chicken is marinating, prepare the Tzatziki sauce. Grate the cucumber (you can peel it but I don't) onto a mesh strainer or paper towel and squeeze out as much liquid as you can, discarding the liquid. Add cucumber to a bowl with yogurt, garlic, dill, lemon juice, salt and pepper. Stir to combine and refrigerate until ready to serve.
4. Grill the chicken. Preheat grill or grill pan to medium-high heat.
5. Remove chicken from the marinade and grill for 8-10 minutes per side, or until a thermometer inserted in the center reads 165°F.
6. Remove chicken from the grill and serve with Tzatziki sauce.

Nutritional Value (Amount per Serving):

Calories: 1102; Fat: 46.78; Carb: 69.44; Protein: 96.14

Instant Pot Chicken and Rice Soup

Prep Time: 25 Mins   Cook Time: 45 Mins   Serves: 4

Ingredients:

- 1 ½ cups low-sodium chicken broth
- ⅓cup brown rice
- 1 ½ pounds chicken breast tenderloins, cubed
- 1 large onion, diced
- 1 ½ cups diced carrot
- 1 ½ cups diced celery
- 1 cup frozen corn kernels
- 1 teaspoon garlic powder
- 1 teaspoon onion powder
- 1 teaspoon poultry seasoning

- ½ teaspoon dried thyme
- ½ teaspoon salt
- ½ teaspoon ground black pepper
- ½ cup half-and-half
- 2 teaspoons cornstarch
- ½ cup frozen peas

Directions:

1. Stir broth and brown rice together in a multi-functional pressure cooker until rice is moistened. Add chicken, onion, carrot, celery, corn, garlic powder, onion powder, poultry seasoning, thyme, salt, and pepper. Close and lock the lid. Select high pressure and set the timer for 18 minutes. Allow 10 to 15 minutes for pressure to build.
2. Release pressure naturally, about 10 minutes. Carefully release remaining pressure using the quick-release method, 2 to 3 minutes. Remove the lid.
3. Stir half-and-half and cornstarch together in a small bowl; stir into the cooker along with frozen peas. Select Sauté function; cook, stirring constantly, until thickened and bubbly, 2 to 3 minutes.

Nutritional Value (Amount per Serving):

Calories: 306; Fat: 4.94; Carb: 31.31; Protein: 35.4

Cousin Cosmos Greek Chicken

Prep Time: 20 Mins   Cook Time: 20 Mins   Serves: 6

Ingredients:

- 2 tablespoons all-purpose flour, divided
- ½ teaspoon salt
- ¼ teaspoon black pepper
- ¼ pound feta cheese, crumbled
- 1 tablespoon fresh lemon juice
- 1 teaspoon dried oregano
- 6 boneless, skinless chicken breast halves
- 2 tablespoons olive oil
- 1 ½ cups water
- 1 cube chicken bouillon, crumbled
- 2 cups loosely packed torn fresh spinach leaves
- 1 ripe tomato, chopped

Directions:

1. On large plate, combine 1 tablespoon flour, salt, and pepper. Set aside. In a small bowl, combine cheese, lemon juice, and oregano. Set aside.
2. With a meat mallet, pound each chicken breast to 1/2 inch thickness. Spread cheese mixture on each chicken breast, leaving 1/2 inch border. Fold chicken breasts in half; secure each with toothpick. Coat chicken

breasts with flour mixture.

3. In large skillet, heat oil over medium heat. Cook chicken breasts for 1 to 2 minutes on each side, until golden. In a small bowl, whisk together 1 1/2 cups water, chicken bouillon cube, and remaining flour; pour over chicken breasts in pan. Add spinach and tomato to skillet, and bring to boil. Cover, reduce heat to low, and simmer for 8 to 10 minutes, or until chicken is no longer pink inside. Discard toothpicks before serving.

Nutritional Value (Amount per Serving):

Calories: 1005; Fat: 38.1; Carb: 111.42; Protein: 52.9

Easy, Healthy Orange Chicken

Prep Time: 10 Mins   Cook Time: 20 Mins   Serves: 4

Ingredients:

- or The Sauce:
- 1 cup 100% orange juice (bottled or fresh squeezed)
- 1 tsp orange zest
- 2 tbsp low-sodium soy sauce
- 2 cloves garlic, minced
- 2 tsp grated fresh ginger or ginger paste
- 1 tsp red pepper flakes
- 1 tbsp corn starch
- 1 tsp sesame oil
- or The Orange Peel Chicken:
- 2 tsp neutral oil, such as avocado oil or canola oil, divided
- 1 1/2 lbs boneless, skinless chicken breast
- Pinch salt and freshly cracked black pepper
- 3 medium carrots, sliced
- 1 cup snow peas
- 1/2 cup frozen edamame, thawed
- or Serving:
- Sliced green onions
- Cooked brown rice, cauliflower rice or quinoa

Directions:

1. Whisk together sauce ingredients and set aside. Chop carrots and cut chicken into bite-sized pieces.
2. Heat a large nonstick skillet over medium heat. Add 1 tsp of the oil. Season chicken with salt and pepper and add to skillet, stirring occasionally so that all sides get browned. Continue cooking until chicken is mostly cooked through, 5-8 minutes. Remove from chicken from skillet and set aside.

3. Add remaining 1 tsp oil to the skillet. Add carrots, snow peas and edamame to skillet and cook, stirring, until carrots are softened, about 5 minutes.

4. Add chicken back to the skillet and pour in sauce. Cook until sauce is thickened, about 5 more minutes.

5. Sprinkle with green onions and serve with cooked brown rice, quinoa, or cauliflower rice.

Nutritional Value (Amount per Serving):

Calories: 413; Fat: 14.39; Carb: 51.23; Protein: 19.8

Chimichurri Chicken Meatballs with Herbed Greek Yogurt, Red Quinoa Green Beans

Prep Time: 25 Mins   Cook Time: 20 Mins   Serves: 6

Ingredients:

- erbed Greek Yogurt
- 1½ cups whole milk plain Greek yogurt
- Juice of 1 small lime
- ¼ cup fresh cilantro leaves
- ¼ cup sliced scallions (green parts only)
- ¼ cup fresh parsley leaves
- 3 or 4 fresh basil leaves
- 1 garlic clove
- 1 teaspoon onion powder
- Kosher salt and freshly ground black pepper, to taste
- uinoa
- 2 cups chicken stock
- 1 cup red quinoa
- ½ cup diced onion
- himichurri Chicken Meatballs
- 1 pound boneless skinless chicken thighs (about 6 thighs)
- ½ cup fresh cilantro
- ½ cup fresh parsley
- ½ small to medium yellow onion
- ¼ cup sliced scallions (green parts only)
- ¼ cup pretzel crumbs
- 3 or 4 basil leaves
- 1 tablespoon fresh lime juice (from ½ a lime)
- 1 egg
- 1 garlic clove
- Kosher salt and freshly ground black pepper, to taste

- Extra-virgin olive oil, as needed
- reen Beans
- 1 tablespoon extra-virgin olive oil
- 1 pound fresh green beans, trimmed and cut
- 2 garlic cloves, chopped
- Kosher salt and freshly ground black pepper, to taste

Directions:

1. MAKE THE YOGURT: Pulse all the ingredients in the bowl of a food processor. Mix for 2 to 3 minutes or until you get the consistency you desire. We like ours pretty smooth. Transfer to a bowl and refrigerate until ready to use.
2. MAKE THE QUINOA: Make the quinoa according to the package instructions, adding the onion, and substituting chicken stock for water, if you have it.
3. MEANWHILE, MAKE THE MEATBALLS: Slice the chicken thighs into thirds. In the bowl of a food processor, combine the chicken, cilantro, parsley, onion, scallions, pretzel crumbs, basil, lime juice, egg, garlic, salt and pepper, and pulse the mixer several times to break up and chop the meat. Pulse until you have a coarse paste.
4. Use a small ½-ounce self-release ice cream scoop to portion the mixture into meatballs—your hands work as well, but the mixture will be very sticky.
5. Heat 2 tablespoons olive oil in a large skillet over medium heat. Fry the meatballs, gently turning them constantly to keep their round shape, until golden brown and cooked through, 6 to 8 minutes. (Do this in batches if you don't have a large enough pan. Don't crowd the pan or they won't caramelize.)
6. MAKE THE GREEN BEANS: Meanwhile, sauté the green beans in olive oil for about 3 minutes over medium-high heat. Add 2 tablespoons water, and cook with the lid on for another 2 to 3 minutes. Remove the lid and add the garlic, salt and pepper. To serve, layer the quinoa, green beans and meatballs in a bowl, then top with yogurt.

Nutritional Value (Amount per Serving):

Calories: 1152; Fat: 43.24; Carb: 29.37; Protein: 152.35

Braised Chicken and Artichoke Hearts with Lemon, Cherry Peppers and Thyme

Prep Time: 20 Mins   Cook Time: 1 Hr 10 Mins   Serves: 4

Ingredients:

- 1 tablespoon olive oil
- 4 chicken leg quarters

- 1 yellow onion, chopped
- 4 cloves garlic, chopped
- 1 tablespoon fresh ground black pepper
- 1 teaspoon salt
- ½ teaspoon red pepper flakes
- 1 quart chicken stock or low-sodium broth
- 10 canned artichoke hearts, drained and halved
- 2 cups cherry peppers
- 2 lemons, juiced
- 8 sprigs fresh thyme
- 1 (16 ounce) can butter beans, drained

Directions:

1. Preheat the oven to 375 degrees F.
2. Coat bottom of a Dutch oven with olive oil and place over high-heat. Sear chicken until browned, about 5 minutes per side. Transfer to a warm plate.
3. Stir onion, garlic, black pepper, salt, and red pepper flakes into the Dutch oven; cook and stir for 1 minute. Stir in chicken broth and return to a simmer. Remove from heat.
4. Return chicken to the Dutch oven. Stir in artichoke hearts, cherry peppers, lemon juice, and thyme.
5. Cover Dutch oven and place in the preheated oven. Cook until chicken is tender, about 1 hour.
6. Remove Dutch oven and transfer chicken to a warm plate.
7. Stir beans into the Dutch oven with broth and artichoke mixture.
8. Serve each chicken leg quarter in a bowl. Pour a ladle-full of artichoke, bean, and broth mixture over each.

Nutritional Value (Amount per Serving):

Calories: 605; Fat: 27.4; Carb: 27.22; Protein: 66.96

Sheet Pan Greek Garlic Butter Chicken and Potatoes

Prep Time: 25 Mins   Cook Time: 45 Mins   Serves: 6

Ingredients:

- 1 pound baby potatoes, halved
- 4 tablespoons plus 1/3 cup extra virgin olive oil
- kosher salt and black pepper
- 2 lemons, 1 halved, and 1 sliced
- 6 chicken thighs or breasts (use similar sizes for even cooking)
- 2 tablespoons dried oregano
- 1 tablespoon smoked or regular paprika

- 1 shallot, chopped
- red pepper flakes
- 6-8 garlic cloves, lightly smashed
- 2 cups mixed fresh parsley, oregano, and dill, chopped
- kosher salt and black pepper
- 1 medium yellow onion, sliced
- 6-8 ounces feta cheese, cubed
- 4 tablespoons salted butter, sliced into 6 pieces
- 2 tablespoons red wine vinegar
- 1-2 pepperoncini, chopped
- 3/4 cup Greek olive mix, or green olives, torn

Directions:

1. Preheat oven to 425°F.
2. On a large baking sheet, toss the potatoes with 2 tablespoons olive oil. Season with salt and black pepper. Add the lemon halves. Roast for 20 minutes, or until tender.
3. In a bowl, toss together 2 tablespoons olive oil, the chicken, dried oregano, paprika, shallot, salt, pepper, and chili flakes.
4. Remove the potatoes from the oven and nestle the chicken around the potatoes. Arrange the onions, garlic, and lemon slices around the chicken. Add 1 slice of butter to each piece of chicken. Return the pan to the oven for 20-25 minutes more, until the chicken is cooked through.
5. To make the dressing. Combine the remaining 1/3 cup olive oil, red wine vinegar, herbs, pepperoncinis, and olives.
6. Remove the charred lemon slices and garlic cloves from the baking sheet. Finely chop the lemon slices, rind and all, discarding any seeds. Add half of the lemon to the dressing. Chop/mash the garlic into a paste, stir the garlic into the dressing. Season with red pepper and salt. Taste adding more of the lemon as desired.
7. Break the feta over the chicken, then add the dressing. Top with fresh herbs. Eat and enjoy!

Nutritional Value (Amount per Serving):

Calories: 1192; Fat: 103.664; Carb: 21.83; Protein: 43.09

Crispy Chicken Schnitzel Recipe

Prep Time: 5 Mins   Cook Time: 8 Mins   Serves: 4

Ingredients:

- 4 boneless skinless chicken breast pieces (about 1 pound and 5 oz)
- Kosher salt and black pepper
- ½ tablespoon garlic powder

- ½ tablespoon sweet paprika
- 1 teaspoon dried oregano
- ½ cup all-purpose flour
- 2 eggs
- 1 ½ cups bread crumbs such as panko bread crumbs
- Extra virgin olive oil
- 1 lemon, juice of

Directions:

1. Put the chicken (one piece at a time) in a large ziptop bag and seal. Using a mallet or the back of a heavy cast iron skillet, pound the chicken. The chicken pieces should be large and quite thin (about ⅛-inch in thickness or so) by the time you're done pounding.
2. Season the chicken with kosher salt and black pepper on both sides. In a small bowl, combine the garlic powder, paprika and oregano then sprinkle the mixture on both sides of the chicken.
3. Preparing a dredging station. Put the flour in one bowl. Beat the eggs in another bowl and place it next to the flour. And put the panko in a third bowl next to the eggs.
4. Take one piece of chicken, and place it in the flour bowl. Coat the chicken on both sides with the flour and shake off excess. Then dip the chicken in the egg bowl. Finally coat the chicken with the panko bread crumbs on both sides. Repeat with the remaining chicken.
5. In a large skillet, heat ½ cup extra virgin olive oil over medium-high heat until shimmering but not smoking. Carefully add the chicken. Cook on one side for 4 minutes or so, then carefully turn over and cook for another 3 to 4 minutes or until golden brown on both sides (if you need to, do this in batches and do not crowd the skillet).
6. Place the fried chicken schnitzel on a tray lined with paper towel to drain excess oil.
7. Squeeze lemon juice on top. Serve with more lemon slices and your choice of salad or side (ideas above)

Nutritional Value (Amount per Serving):

Calories: 515; Fat: 13.87; Carb: 26.09; Protein: 68.33

Lemon Chicken Orzo Soup

Prep Time: 20 Mins   Cook Time: 1 Hr   Serves: 12

Ingredients:

- 8 ounces orzo pasta
- 1 teaspoon olive oil

- 3 medium carrots, chopped, or more to taste
- 3 ribs celery, chopped
- 1 medium onion, chopped
- 2 cloves garlic, minced
- ½ teaspoon dried thyme
- ½ teaspoon dried oregano
- salt and ground black pepper to taste
- 1 bay leaf
- 3 (32 ounce) cartons fat-free, low-sodium chicken broth
- ½ cup fresh lemon juice
- 1 lemon, zested
- 8 ounces cooked chicken breast, chopped
- 1 (8 ounce) package baby spinach leaves
- 1 lemon, sliced for garnish (Optional)
- ¼ cup grated Parmesan cheese (Optional)

Directions:

1. Bring a large pot of lightly salted water to a boil. Stir in orzo and return to a boil. Cook pasta uncovered until partially cooked through but not yet soft, about 5 minutes; drain and rinse with cold water until cooled completely.
2. Heat olive oil in a large pot over medium heat. Add carrots, celery, and onion; cook and stir until vegetables begin to soften and onion becomes translucent, 5 to 7 minutes. Add garlic; cook and stir until fragrant, about 1 minute more. Season mixture with thyme, oregano, bay leaf, salt, and black pepper; continue cooking another 30 seconds before pouring chicken broth into the pot.
3. Bring broth to a boil. Partially cover the pot, reduce heat to medium-low, and simmer until vegetables are just tender, about 10 minutes.
4. Stir orzo, lemon juice, and lemon zest into broth; add chicken. Cook until chicken and orzo are heated through, about 5 minutes. Add baby spinach; cook until spinach wilts into broth and orzo is tender, 2 to 3 minutes. Ladle soup into bowls; garnish with lemon slices and Parmesan cheese.

Nutritional Value (Amount per Serving):

Calories: 98; Fat: 2.03; Carb: 12.37; Protein: 8.36

Skinny Slow Cooker Kale and Turkey Meatball Soup

Prep Time: 15 Mins   Cook Time: 4 Hrs   Serves: 8

Ingredients:

- ¼ cup milk
- 2 slices bread

- 1 pound lean ground turkey , (85% lean)
- 1 medium shallot , finely chopped
- 2 cloves garlic , finely chopped
- ½ teaspoon freshly grated nutmeg
- 1 teaspoon oregano
- ¼ teaspoon red pepper flakes
- kosher salt and freshly ground pepper
- ½ cup Parmigiano-Reggiano , grated, plus more for serving
- 2 tablespoons Italian parsley , chopped
- 1 egg , beaten
- 1 tablespoon olive oil
- 8 cups chicken or vegetable broth , (64 ounces)
- 1 15- ounce can white Northern beans or other small white bean , drained and rinsed
- 2 carrots , sliced
- ½ yellow onion , chopped
- 4 cups kale about 1 pound

Directions:

1. Add milk to a large mixing bowl then tear the bread into chunks and add to the milk to soak. Add the turkey, shallot, garlic, nutmeg, oregano, red pepper flakes, salt and pepper, cheese, parsley and egg and gently mix with your fingers until the mixture is combined. Use a small scoop or melon baller to form ½ inch balls.
2. Heat the olive oil in a large skillet over medium high heat and lightly sear the meatballs for 1-2 minutes on each side. Remove from the pan and set aside.
3. Add the broth, beans, carrots, onion and kale to the insert of a 5- to 7-quart slow cooker.
4. Drop the meatballs onto the kale, cover and cook on low for 4 hours or until the meatballs float to the surface.
5. Serve the soup garnished with grated parmesan cheese, red pepper flakes and fresh parsley leaves.

Nutritional Value (Amount per Serving):

Calories: 674; Fat: 35.29; Carb: 8.09; Protein: 76.8

Grilled Spatchcocked Greek Chicken

Prep Time: 15 Mins   Cook Time: 1 Hr 10 Mins   Serves: 6

Ingredients:

- 1 cup extra virgin olive oil

- ¼ cup lemon juice
- 3 tablespoons chopped fresh oregano
- 3 cloves garlic, minced
- 2 teaspoons minced fresh rosemary
- 1 teaspoon dried tarragon
- 1 (4.5 pound) whole chicken, spatchcocked
- salt and ground black pepper to taste

Directions:

1. Whisk olive oil, lemon juice, oregano, garlic, rosemary, and tarragon together in a measuring cup.
2. Preheat an outdoor grill for medium-high heat and lightly oil the grate.
3. Place chicken on a rimmed baking sheet. Pour 1/2 of the oil mixture over the chicken and reserve the remaining 1/2. Using your hands, massage the oil mixture into the chicken skin. Season with salt and pepper.
4. Grill chicken skin-side up over indirect heat for 50 minutes. Move chicken over direct heat and grill 5 minutes. Carefully flip chicken over skin-side down and grill until skin is brown and crispy, about 5 more minutes. Transfer chicken to a serving platter and let rest for 10 minutes.
5. Drizzle reserved oil mixture over the chicken. Carve and serve.

Nutritional Value (Amount per Serving):

Calories: 208; Fat: 17.57; Carb: 8.01; Protein: 5.16

Chicken Pan Pie

Prep Time: 20 Mins   Cook Time: 1 Hr 5 Mins   Serves: 6

Ingredients:

- ¼ cup unsalted butter
- ⅔cup diced onion
- ½ teaspoon kosher salt, or to taste
- 1 ½ pounds boneless, skinless chicken thighs, cut into 1-inch pieces
- ¼ cup all-purpose flour
- 2 ½ cups chicken broth
- ½ cup sliced carrots
- ½ cup sliced celery
- ¼ teaspoon freshly ground black pepper
- 1 pinch cayenne pepper
- ½ cup frozen peas, thawed
- 1 teaspoon fresh thyme leaves
- 1 recipe pastry pie dough
- 1 large egg, beaten
- 2 teaspoons water

Directions:

1. Gather all ingredients. Preheat the oven to 425 degrees F.
2. Melt butter in a 12-inch cast iron skillet over medium-high heat. Add diced onion and salt. Cook, stirring, until onions start to soften, and the edges begin to brown, 3 to 4 minutes.

3. Add chicken, and cook, stirring, until the chicken loses its pink color, and starts to brown in spots, 3 to 4 minutes.
4. Sprinkle flour over top, then cook and stir for about 2 minutes. Pour in the broth and bring to a simmer, scraping the bottom of the pan with a spatula. Stir in carrots, celery, black pepper, and cayenne.
5. Cook the mixture, stirring occasionally, until it's as thick as you want, 5 to 10 minutes. For a thick, sticky filling once baked, reduce until the sauce coats the back of a spoon. For a saucier filling, don't reduce the mixture at all.
6. Turn off the heat and stir in the peas and thyme. Taste for seasoning and reserve until needed.
7. Roll out pie or pastry dough to form a circle about 14 inches in diameter.
8. Fold over 1/2 inch of dough all the way around, and then crimp the edge to make a decorative scalloped design. Cut or punch out a 1-inch hole in the center of the dough.
9. Place the pan on top of a sheet pan in case filling bubbles over in the oven. Carefully place the dough over the filling, and adjust until it's centered. Press the crust lightly into the filling. Brush the top with an egg wash if desired.
10. Bake in the preheated oven until crust is browned and filling is bubbling, about 40 minutes. Let rest for 5 minutes before serving.
11. Serve and enjoy!

Nutritional Value (Amount per Serving):

Calories: 651; Fat: 31.58; Carb: 50.93; Protein: 38.59

Chapter 7: Beef, Pork, and Lamb

Braised Lamb with Radishes and Mint

Prep Time: 10 Mins   Cook Time: 3 Hrs 33 Mins   Serves: 4

Ingredients:

- 1 tablespoon kosher salt
- 1 teaspoon black pepper
- 1 teaspoon paprika
- ¼ teaspoon cayenne pepper
- 4 (10 ounce) lamb shoulder chops
- 1 tablespoon olive oil
- ⅓ cup sherry vinegar
- 2 tablespoons white sugar
- 4 oil-packed anchovy fillets
- 1 ½ cups low-sodium chicken broth
- 2 teaspoons minced fresh rosemary
- ¼ teaspoon ground cinnamon
- 2 bunches breakfast radishes, rinsed and trimmed
- 5 fresh mint leaves, finely sliced
- 1 tablespoon cold butter

Directions:

1. Preheat oven to 275 degrees F.
2. Mix together salt, pepper, paprika, and cayenne pepper. Place lamb chops on a work surface; press seasoning onto both sides of lamb chops.
3. Heat oil in large oven-proof skillet over high heat. Brown lamb well on both sides, 3 or 4 minutes per side. Remove chops from pan; reduce heat to low. Add vinegar, sugar, and anchovies. Cook and stir, breaking up anchovies. Turn up heat to medium and continue stirring until mixture reduces to the consistency of syrup, about 3 minutes. Stir in chicken broth. Raise heat to high. Add rosemary and cinnamon; bring to a simmer. Transfer browned lamb chops to pan and place radishes among the chops. Cover.
4. Place skillet in preheated oven. Roast slowly for 1 1/2 hours; turn chops. Continue roasting until meat is just tender and is beginning to separate from the bone, about 1 1/2 additional hours. Turn chops again.
5. Raise oven temperature to 425 degrees F. Remove cover from skillet. Roast until meat is falling off the bone and fork tender, 15 to 20 minutes. Remove skillet from oven.
6. Transfer lamb and radishes to serving platter. Place pan on stove over medium-high heat. Bring sauce to a simmer until it is slightly reduced and thickened, skimming off surface fat. Remove from heat. Add sliced mint and butter. Keep stirring until butter melts. Spoon sauce over lamb and radishes.

Nutritional Value (Amount per Serving):

Calories: 993; Fat: 62.55; Carb: 11.62; Protein: 99.08

Heavenly Meatloaf with Blue Cheese, Mushrooms, and Spinach

Prep Time: 15 Mins   Cook Time: 45 Mins   Serves: 8

Ingredients:

- 2 eggs
- 1 cup finely chopped fresh spinach
- ½ cup sliced fresh mushrooms
- ½ cup plain bread crumbs
- ½ small yellow onion, finely chopped
- ⅓cup 2% milk
- ⅓cup crumbled blue cheese
- 2 tablespoons reduced-sodium Worcestershire sauce
- 1 tablespoon minced garlic
- ¼ teaspoon cayenne pepper
- 1 pinch dried oregano
- 1 pinch dried basil
- salt and ground black pepper to taste
- 1 ½ pounds extra-lean ground beef

Directions:

1. Preheat the oven to 350 degrees F. Grease a loaf pan.
2. Mix eggs, spinach, mushrooms, bread crumbs, onion, milk, blue cheese, Worcestershire sauce, garlic, cayenne pepper, oregano, basil, salt, and black pepper together in a large bowl. Add ground beef and mix thoroughly with your hands; pack into the prepared loaf pan.
3. Bake in the preheated oven until no longer pink in the center, 45 to 60 minutes. An instant-read thermometer inserted into the center should read at least 160 degrees F.

Nutritional Value (Amount per Serving):

Calories: 302; Fat: 17.26; Carb: 8.8; Protein: 26.69

Mediterranean Grilled Lamb Chop Recipe With Tomato Mint Quinoa

Prep Time: 10 Mins   Cook Time: 55 Mins   Serves: 6 To 8

Ingredients:

- or The Lamb
- 1 tsp garlic paste (or finely minced garlic)
- 1 tsp allspice
- 1/2 tsp ground green cardamom
- 1/2 tsp ground nutmeg
- 1/4 tsp sweet paprika
- 1/2 tsp salt
- scant 1 tsp black pepper
- 1 tbsp chopped fresh mint leaves
- Olive oil
- 2 frenched racks of lamb, fat trimmed, separated into chops (about 16 chops)

- 1 large lemon, juice of
- 1 small yellow or red onion, sliced
- or The Tomato Mint Quinoa
- 1 cup dry quinoa, rinsed
- water
- 2 tbsp olive oil
- 3 garlic cloves, chopped
- 1 14.5 oz can petit tomato diced
- Salt and pepper
- 1 cup chopped fresh mint leaves, more for garnish
- 1/2 cup finely chopped red onion
- 1/3 cup crumbled feta cheese

Directions:

1. In a small bowl combine the garlic and spices with 1 tbsp fresh mint leaves and 2 tbsp of olive oil. This makes a rub for the lamb.
2. Take the lamb chops and rub them each on both sides with the garlic-spice rub. Place the chops in a deep dish with 2 tbsp olive oil, lemon juice and onions. Cover and leave in the fridge for 1 to 4 hours.
3. 20 to 25 minutes before grilling, remove the lamb chops from the fridge and let them rest at room temperature.
4. Meanwhile, cook the quinoa according to package instructions, adding a dash of salt and olive oil to the cooking water. (For 1 cup of quinoa, you'll add 3 cups of water. Bring to a boil, then cover, reduce heat to medium low and simmer until water is absorbed, 15 to 20 minutes.)
5. Now let's add flavor to the cooked quinoa! In a non-stick pan, heat 2 tbsp olive oil over medium heat. Stir in garlic and cook very briefly and then add the canned diced tomato. Season with salt and pepper and cook for 4-6 minutes, stirring occasionally. Now, stir in the cooked quinoa. Once warmed through, add the chopped fresh mint. Stir to combine and remove from heat. Off heat, add chopped red onions, feta cheese and more fresh mint leaves for garnish
6. Time to grill the lamb chops! Heat an a gas grill (or an indoor grill pan) over high heat (make sure the grill is super hot) add the lamb chops and grill for about 2 minutes. Flip the chops over and cook for another 3 minutes for medium-rare or 3 1/2 minutes for medium (internal temperature should register 125 degrees F for medium-rare or 135 degrees F for medium). Let the chops rest for 10 minutes before serving.
7. When ready to serve, transfer the tomato mint quinoa to serving bowls, top with 2 lamb chops per person. Enjoy!

Nutritional Value (Amount per Serving):

Calories: 256; Fat: 13.34; Carb: 22.92; Protein: 12.72

Shredded Beef Enchiladas

Prep Time: 15 Mins   Cook Time: 25 Mins   Serves: 8

Ingredients:

- 2 cups red enchilada sauce
- 1 1/2 pounds cooked beef, shredded
- 2 1/2 cups cheddar cheese or Monterey Jack cheese, shredded
- 8 medium flour tortillas, 8-inches in diameter
- or Serving (Optional):
- fresh cilantro, chopped
- sour cream
- lime juice, freshly squeezed
- guacamole
- pico de gallo

Directions:

1. Preheat oven to 350 F.
2. Spread 1/4 cup enchilada sauce onto a 9x13-inch casserole pan. Set aside.
3. On each tortilla, spread 1-2 tablespoons of enchilada sauce on the bottom. Add 1/3 cup shredded beef and 2 tablespoons cheese on top in the centre. Carefully roll the tortilla up and arrange it seam side down into the casserole pan. Repeat with the remaining filling and tortillas
4. Spread the remaining enchilada sauce evenly on top and sprinkle with the remaining cheese.
5. Cover the pan with aluminum foil and bake for 15 minutes. Remove the cover and bake uncovered for another 8-10 minutes until the melted cheese turns golden brown. Let rest for 5 minutes.
6. Serve warm with cilantro, sour cream, and lime juice if desired.

Nutritional Value (Amount per Serving):

Calories: 668; Fat: 30.36; Carb: 48.81; Protein: 51.32

Soutzoukakia (Greek Baked Meatballs)

Prep Time: 20 Mins   Cook Time: 1 Hr 40 Mins   Serves: 16

Ingredients:

- or Meatballs
- 2 slices whole wheat bread, toast-size, toasted to a medium-brown (or use gluten free bread if you need)
- ⅓cup whole milk
- 1.5 pounds lean ground beef
- 1 small yellow onion, chopped
- 3 garlic cloves, minced
- 2 medium eggs
- 1 teaspoon ground cumin

- ½ teaspoon ground cinnamon
- ½ teaspoon dried oregano
- ½ cup chopped fresh parsley
- Kosher salt and black pepper
- Extra virgin olive oil, to grease the baking dish
- or Red Sauce
- 2 tablespoons Extra virgin olive oil
- 1 medium yellow onion, finely chopped
- 2 garlic cloves, minced
- ½ cup dry red wine
- 30 ounces canned tomato sauce, that's 2 15-ounce cans of sauce
- 1 bay leaf
- ¾ teaspoon ground cumin
- ½ teaspoon cinnamon
- ½ teaspoon sugar
- Kosher salt and black pepper

Directions:

1. In a small bowl, place the toasted bread and cover with milk (or water) to soak. When bread is soft and well-soaked, squeeze the liquid out completely and discard remaining milk if any.
2. Transfer the bread to a large mixing bowl. Add round beef and remaining meatball ingredients. Knead well until well-combined. Cover the meat mixture and rest in the fridge for now.
3. Preheat oven to 400°F.
4. While oven is heating, prepare the sauce. In a sauce pan or large skillet, heat 2 tablespoon of extra virgin olive oil over medium heat until shimmering but not smoking. Add onions and cook for 3 minutes or so. Add garlic and cook for another minute, stirring regularly. Now add red wine and cook to reduce by about ½, then add tomato sauce, bay leaf and remaining sauce ingredients. Bring to a boil, then lower heat and simmer for 15 minutes.
5. Prepare a large baking dish and lightly oil the bottom with extra virgin olive oil.
6. Take the meat mixture out of the fridge. Wet your hands and scoop portions of about 2 ½ tablespoon of the meat mixture and form into large elongated meatballs (football-shaped.) You should have 15 to 16 meatballs or so. Arrange meatballs in the papered baking dish and top with the sauce (be sure to have removed the bay leaf from the sauce.)
7. Place the baking dish on the middle rack of your heated oven. Bake for 40 to 45 minutes or until the meatballs are well cooked through (check part-way through to make sure sauce is not dry, and if needed, add a little bit of water to the bottom of the baking dish.)
8. Remove from oven and add another drizzle of EVOO. Garnish with parsley

and serve over rice or orzo.

Nutritional Value (Amount per Serving):

Calories: 155; Fat: 6.96; Carb: 9.3; Protein: 13.78

Lamb Ragu

Prep Time: 10 Mins   Cook Time: 3 Hrs   Serves: 6-8

Ingredients:

- 2 Tbsp olive oil
- 2 small carrots, peeled and diced
- 2 celery stalks, diced
- 1 medium onion, diced
- 5-6 garlic cloves
- 2 pounds ground lamb
- 2 Tbsp tomato paste
- 1 cup red wine
- 28oz crushed tomatoes
- 1 cup beef stock
- 1 sprig fresh rosemary
- 7-8 sprigs fresh thyme
- 1 tsp dried oregano
- 2 bay leaves
- salt to taste
- pepper to taste
- sugar to taste

Directions:

1. Heat olive oil in a large pot over medium heat. Add the diced onion, celery and carrot, then reduce heat to low. Sauté till the vegetables become soft, without browning them.
2. Add in the lamb, along with garlic, and break it up with a wooden spoon. Cook till it is no longer pink.
3. Stir in the tomato paste and cook it for 2-3 minutes.
4. Add wine and deglaze the pan. Simmer for 4-5 minutes, to allow the wine to reduce a bit.
5. Add in your crushed tomatoes, beef stock and herbs. Stir until well combined.
6. Bring the sauce to a low boil, then reduce heat to medium low. Allow to simmer uncovered for at least 2-3 hours. If the sauce begins to get too thick, stir in more water. Taste and adjust for salt, pepper and sugar.
7. Toss with your favorite pasta, garnish with parsley and freshly grated parmesan cheese.

Nutritional Value (Amount per Serving):

Calories: 691; Fat: 32.01; Carb: 36.65; Protein: 69.87

Instant Pot Mongolian Beef

Prep Time: 10 Mins   Cook Time: 50 Mins   Serves: 8

Ingredients:

- 1 head garlic
- 2 pounds flank steak
- salt and ground black pepper to taste
- 1 tablespoon olive oil
- 2 sweet onions, cut into wedges
- ⅔cup dark brown sugar
- ½ cup water
- 1 green bell pepper, sliced
- 1 red bell pepper, sliced
- ½ cup liquid amino acid
- ½ teaspoon minced fresh ginger root
- 3 tablespoons water
- 2 tablespoons arrowroot powder
- 3 green onions, cut in 1-inch pieces

Directions:

1. Preheat the oven to 350 degrees F.
2. Brush unpeeled garlic cloves with a small amount of olive oil and wrap in a piece of aluminum foil.
3. Bake in the preheated oven until garlic cloves are tender and browned, about 20 minutes. Let cool; remove skin from cloves.
4. Season steak with salt and pepper. Add oil to a multi-functional pressure cooker and select Saute function. Cook steak in batches until browned, about 8 minutes. Do not crowd the pot. Transfer beef to a plate.
5. Saute garlic in the pot until fragrant, about 1 minute. Add onions, brown sugar, 1/2 cup water, green bell pepper, red bell pepper, liquid aminos, and ginger. Stir to combine. Add browned beef and any accumulated juices.
6. Close and lock the lid. Select high pressure according to manufacturer's instructions; set timer for 12 minutes. Allow 10 to 15 minutes for pressure to build.
7. Release pressure carefully using the quick-release method according to manufacturer's instructions, about 5 minutes. Unlock and remove the lid.
8. Combine 3 tablespoons water and arrowroot powder in a bowl; whisk until smooth. Add mixture to the sauce in the pot, stirring constantly. Select Simmer mode and bring to a boil; stir constantly until sauce thickens, about 5 minutes. Stir in green onions.

Nutritional Value (Amount per Serving):

Calories: 285; Fat: 7.67; Carb: 27.6; Protein: 26.67

Instant Pot Sauerkraut Soup with Sausage

Prep Time: 25 Mins   Cook Time: 30 Mins   Serves: 6

Ingredients:

- 12 ounces smoked sausage, chopped
- 1 large onion, chopped
- 2 ribs celery, sliced
- 1 tablespoon minced garlic
- 3 sprigs fresh thyme, leaves only
- ½ teaspoon ground black pepper

- 2 (14.5 ounce) cans sauerkraut, drained
- 1 pound red potatoes, cubed
- 5 cups chicken broth
- 6 fluid ounces hard apple cider

Directions:

1. Turn on a multi-functional pressure cooker and select Saute function. Add sausage and cook until caramelized and fat is rendered, about 4 minutes. Add onion, celery, garlic, thyme leaves, and pepper. Cook for 3 more minutes. Cancel Saute mode.
2. Add sauerkraut, potatoes, chicken broth, and hard cider to the pot. Close and lock the lid. Select High pressure according to manufacturer's instructions; set timer for 8 minutes. Allow 10 minutes for pressure to build.
3. Release pressure carefully using the quick-release method according to manufacturer's instructions, about 5 minutes.

Nutritional Value (Amount per Serving):

Calories: 582; Fat: 24.81; Carb: 34.86; Protein: 57.64

Chapter 8: Vegetable

Blistered Green Beans with Tomatoes, Pounded Walnuts and Raw Summer Squash

Prep Time: 10 Mins   Cook Time: 10 Mins   Serves: 4

Ingredients:

- 1 cup walnuts, toasted
- ½ bunch parsley, roughly chopped
- Zest and juice of 1 lemon
- ¼ cup olive oil
- Kosher salt
- 1 tablespoon neutral oil, like canola
- 1 pound green beans, stems snapped off
- 1 pint cherry tomatoes, halved
- 1 medium summer squash, shaved into paper-thin planks or rounds

Directions:

1. Place the walnuts in a ziplock plastic bag and bash with the bottom of a frying pan until the walnuts are broken into coarse pieces and have released some oil.
2. Combine the walnuts, parsley, lemon zest and juice, olive oil and a pinch of salt, and stir to combine.
3. Heat the neutral oil until smoking hot and add the green beans with a pinch of salt. Let the green beans blister, then toss to coat, flip and blister the other side.
4. Remove from the heat and toss with the tomatoes and summer squash. Top with the walnut mixture and serve.

Nutritional Value (Amount per Serving):

Calories: 320; Fat: 30.64; Carb: 10.91; Protein: 5.2

Slow Cooker Lemon Basil Ratatouille

Prep Time: 10 Mins   Cook Time: 5 Hrs   Serves: 8

Ingredients:

- 1 small eggplant
- 2 medium sized zucchini
- 2 medium sized summer squash
- 1 large white onion
- 2 cups cherry or grape tomatoes
- 1 cup loosely packed basil
- 1/3 cup olive oil
- Juice of 1 lemon
- 3 cloves garlic minced
- 2 tbsp tomato paste
- 2 tbsp white wine vinegar
- 1 tsp salt plus more to taste

Directions:

1. Begin by chopping your vegetables into small chunks. Keep the tomatoes whole.

For The Slow Cooker:

1. Place all vegetables inside the bottom of your slow cooker.
2. Blend together, basil, olive oil, lemon, garlic, tomato paste, vinegar, and salt in a food processor or blender until the basil is completely pureed and incorporated. Toss on top of the vegetables.
3. Cook on low for 5-6 hours.
4. Serve hot with extra basil for garnish, and salt to taste.

For The Instant Pot:

1. Place all vegetables inside the bottom of your Instant Pot.
2. Blend together, basil, olive oil, lemon, garlic, tomato paste, vinegar, and salt in a food processor or blender until the basil is completely pureed and incorporated. Toss on top of the vegetables.
3. Secure the lid on your Instant Pot. Select the manual function. Cook on high pressure for 10 minutes. Once complete, use a natural release.
4. Serve hot with extra basil for garnish and salt to taste. Serve as a side dish, or over your favorite pasta or spiralized vegetable noodles.

Nutritional Value (Amount per Serving):

Calories: 140; Fat: 10.24; Carb: 11.77; Protein: 2.08

Instant Pot Spicy Black Bean Soup (Vegan)

Prep Time: 20 Mins   Cook Time: 55 Mins   Serves: 8

Ingredients:

- 2 tablespoons olive oil
- 1 medium white onion, chopped
- 1 yellow bell pepper, diced
- 5 cloves garlic, crushed
- 4 teaspoons chili powder
- 1 ½ teaspoons ground cumin
- 1 ½ teaspoons dried oregano
- ½ teaspoon salt
- ½ teaspoon freshly ground black pepper
- ¼ teaspoon chipotle pepper powder
- 6 cups vegetable broth
- 1 pound dry black beans
- 1 (4 ounce) can chopped Hatch chile peppers, undrained
- 1 pinch garlic salt, or to taste

- Garnish:
- 1 cup pico de gallo
- 1 red bell pepper, sliced
- 1 lime, cut into wedges

Directions:

1. Turn on a multi-functional pressure cooker (such as Instant Pot) and select Saute function. Add oil and heat until shimmering. Add onion and yellow pepper; cook and stir until translucent and soft, about 5 minutes.
2. Add garlic, chili powder, cumin, oregano, salt, pepper, and chipotle powder. Stir until fragrant, about 1 minute. Add broth, beans, and chile peppers. Close and lock the lid. Select high pressure according to manufacturer's instructions; set timer for 40 minutes. Allow 10 to 15 minutes for pressure to build.
3. Release pressure using the natural-release method according to manufacturer's instructions, about 25 minutes. Unlock and remove the lid. Use a stick blender to blend beans until thick and creamy. Season with garlic salt. Serve with pico de gallo, red bell pepper slices, and lime wedges.

Nutritional Value (Amount per Serving):

Calories: 225; Fat: 9.03; Carb: 27.19; Protein: 10.85

Spiralized Ratatouille

Prep Time: 25 Mins   Cook Time: 30 Mins   Serves: 4

Ingredients:

- 2 tablespoons olive oil
- 2 large garlic cloves, pressed or minced
- 1/4 teaspoon red pepper flakes
- 1 sweet yellow (Vidalia) onion, peeled, spiralized with blade A, noodles trimmed
- 2 red bell peppers, spiralized with blade A, noodles trimmed
- 1 medium zucchini, spiralized with blade D, noodles trimmed
- 1 medium yellow squash, spiralized with blade A, noodles trimmed
- 1 cup packed julienned eggplant (from 1 small eggplant; you'll have leftovers)
- Salt
- Freshly ground black pepper
- 1 large can (28 ounces) whole peeled tomatoes, with their juices
- 1 bay leaf
- 1 tablespoon fresh oregano leaves or 1 teaspoon dried oregano
- 1/4 cup packed fresh basil, finely chopped

Directions:

1. In a large pot or Dutch oven over medium heat, warm the oil until shimmering. Add the garlic, red pepper flakes and onion. Cook, stirring often, until the onion is softened, about 5 minutes.
2. Add the bell pepper, zucchini, squash noodles and eggplant. Season with salt and pepper and cook until the vegetables are softened, about 7 to 10 minutes.
3. Crush the tomatoes individually by hand over the pot (beware of red splashes!), adding each one to the pot, as well as all of the juices remaining in the can. Stir in the bay leaf and oregano. Increase the heat to high and bring the mixture to a boil, then reduce heat to low and simmer until the vegetables are tender, 7 to 15 minutes (take care not to overcook them, or they'll be mushy).
4. Stir in the basil and cook for 1 more minute. Remove the bay leaf before serving.

Nutritional Value (Amount per Serving):

Calories: 407; Fat: 24.96; Carb: 22.43; Protein: 24.31

Mediterranean Cauliflower Rice

Prep Time: 20 Mins   Cook Time: 15 Mins   Serves: 4

Ingredients:

- 1 medium-to-large head cauliflower or 16 ounces store-bought cauliflower rice
- 1/2 cup sliced almonds
- 2 tablespoons extra-virgin olive oil
- 2 cloves garlic, pressed or minced
- Pinch of red pepper flakes (omit if sensitive to spice)
- 1/4 teaspoon fine sea salt
- 1/2 cup chopped flat-leaf parsley
- 1 tablespoon lemon juice
- Freshly ground black pepper, to taste

Directions:

1. If you're working with a head of cauliflower, cut it into medium chunks (see photo) and discard the core. Working in batches, pulse the chunks in a food processor with the S-blade until they're broken into tiny pieces, just bigger than couscous. (See recipe notes if you don't have a food processor.)
2. Wrap the cauliflower rice in a clean tea towel or paper towels, twist, and squeeze as much water as possible from the rice—you might be surprised by how much water you can wring out.

3. Toast the almonds in a large skillet over medium heat, stirring frequently (careful, or they'll burn), until they're fragrant and starting to turn golden on the edges, about 3 to 5 minutes. Transfer the toasted almonds to a bowl to cool.

4. Return the skillet to the heat and add the olive oil and garlic. Cook while stirring until the garlic is fragrant, about 10 to 20 seconds. Add the cauliflower rice, red pepper flakes and salt, and stir to combine. Cook, stirring just every minute or so, until the cauliflower rice is hot and turning golden in places, about 6 to 10 minutes.

5. Remove the skillet from the heat. Stir in the toasted almonds, parsley and lemon juice. Season to taste with salt and pepper, and serve warm.

Nutritional Value (Amount per Serving):

Calories: 279; Fat: 19.84; Carb: 3.04; Protein: 21.34

Vegan Green Bean, Tomato, and Basil Sheet Pan Dinner

Prep Time: 10 Mins   Cook Time: 45 Mins   Serves: 4

Ingredients:

- 2 cups baby potatoes
- 3 tablespoons olive oil, divided (Optional)
- 2 cups cherry tomatoes
- 2 cups 1-inch cut fresh green beans
- 4 cloves garlic, minced
- 2 teaspoons dried basil
- 1 teaspoon flaked sea salt (such as Maldon)
- 1 (15 ounce) can garbanzo beans, drained and rinsed
- 2 teaspoons olive oil, or to taste (Optional)
- salt and ground black pepper to taste

Directions:

1. Preheat the oven to 425 degrees F. Line a jelly roll pan with aluminum foil.
2. Toss potatoes with 1 tablespoon olive oil in a medium bowl. Pour into the prepared pan.
3. Roast in the preheated oven until tender, about 30 minutes.
4. Toss cherry tomatoes, green beans, garlic, basil, and sea salt with 2 tablespoons olive oil.
5. Remove potatoes from the oven, push them to one side of the pan, and add the tomato and green bean mixture. Roast until tomatoes start to wilt, 15 to 20 more minutes.
6. Remove from the oven and pour into a serving dish. Stir in garbanzo

beans, add 2 teaspoons olive oil, and season with salt and pepper.

Nutritional Value (Amount per Serving):

Calories: 301; Fat: 14.25; Carb: 37.3; Protein: 7.8

Mediterranean Spinach Beans

Prep Time: 10 Mins   Cook Time: 20 Mins   Serves: 4

Ingredients:

- 1 tablespoon olive oil
- 1 small onion, chopped
- 2 garlic cloves, minced
- 1 can (14-1/2 ounces) no-salt-added diced tomatoes, undrained
- 2 tablespoons Worcestershire sauce
- 1/4 teaspoon salt
- 1/4 teaspoon pepper
- 1/8 teaspoon crushed red pepper flakes
- 1 can (15 ounces) cannellini beans, rinsed and drained
- 1 can (14 ounces) water-packed artichoke hearts, rinsed, drained and quartered
- 6 ounces fresh baby spinach (about 8 cups)
- Additional olive oil, optional

Directions:

1. In a 12-in. skillet, heat oil over medium-high heat; saute onion until tender, 3-5 minutes. Add garlic; cook and stir 1 minute. Stir in tomatoes, Worcestershire sauce and seasonings; bring to a boil. Reduce heat; simmer, uncovered, until liquid is almost evaporated, 6-8 minutes.
2. Add beans, artichoke hearts and spinach; cook and stir until spinach is wilted, 3-5 minutes. If desired, drizzle with additional oil.

Nutritional Value (Amount per Serving):

Calories: 98; Fat: 7.08; Carb: 8.26; Protein: 1.98

Fall Instant Pot Shakshuka

Prep Time: 15 Mins   Cook Time: 30 Mins   Serves: 4

Ingredients:

- 1 tablespoon olive oil
- 1 cup diced yellow onion (about 1/2 large onion)
- 1 green bell pepper, diced

- 1/4 teaspoon salt
- 1/4 teaspoon black pepper
- 1 garlic clove, minced
- 2 cups diced butternut squash (1/2-inch cubes)
- 1 28- ounce can whole plum tomatoes (with juice), coarsely chopped
- 1 teaspoon chili powder
- 1/2 teaspoon smoked paprika
- 1/2 teaspoon dried oregano
- 1/4 teaspoon red pepper flakes
- 2 tablespoons minced fresh parsley, additional for garnishing
- 4 Nellie's Free Range Eggs
- 1/4 cup crumbled feta
- 1 tablespoon shelled pumpkin seeds (pepitas)
- Bread for serving

Directions:

1. Heat Instant Pot to "sauté" and add olive oil. Add onion, bell pepper, salt, and pepper. Cook, stirring, for 4-5 minutes or until onions are soft and translucent. Add garlic and continue to cook, stirring, for about 1 minute or until garlic is fragrant.
2. Add squash, tomatoes, chili powder, smoked paprika, oregano, and red pepper flakes. Stir to combine.
3. Place cover on pressure cooker and set valve to "seal." Cook on high pressure (manual setting) for 8 minutes. Quick release pressure and remove lid.
4. Stir in parsley. Add Nellie's Free Range eggs (see notes). Replace cover, set valve to "seal." Cook on high pressure (manual setting) for 0 minutes (ZERO minutes - not a typo!). Quick release pressure and remove lid.
5. Serve immediately (see note about yolks) topped with feta, pumpkin seeds, and additional parsley. We love to serve it with bread for dipping.

Nutritional Value (Amount per Serving):

Calories: 282; Fat: 18.78; Carb: 16.78; Protein: 12.81

Lemon-Roasted Mixed Vegetables

Prep Time: 10 Mins   Cook Time: 25 Mins   Serves: 5

Ingredients:

- 1 ½ cups cauliflower florets
- 1 ½ cups broccoli florets
- 2 cloves garlic, thinly sliced
- 1 tablespoon olive oil

- 1 teaspoon dried oregano, crushed
- ¼ teaspoon salt
- ¾ cup diced red bell pepper (1-inch)
- ¾ cup diced zucchini (1-inch)
- 2 teaspoons lemon zest

Directions:

1. Preheat oven to 425 degrees F.
2. Combine cauliflower, broccoli, and garlic in a 15-by-10-inch baking pan. Drizzle with oil and sprinkle with oregano and salt; stir to coat. Roast for 10 minutes.
3. Add bell pepper and zucchini to the vegetables in the pan; stir to combine. Roast until the vegetables are crisp-tender and lightly browned, 10 to 15 minutes more.
4. Sprinkle lemon zest over the vegetables; stir and serve.

Nutritional Value (Amount per Serving):

Calories: 40; Fat: 2.89; Carb: 3.3; Protein: 1.28

Easy Brown Rice Pilaf with Spring Vegetables

Prep Time: 30 Mins   Cook Time: 30 Mins   Serves: 4

Ingredients:

- 2 (10 ounce) packages steamable frozen spring vegetables
- 2 cups cooked brown rice (see associated recipe)
- 1 (15 ounce) can no-salt-added chickpeas, rinsed
- 2 tablespoons extra-virgin olive oil
- ½ teaspoon salt
- ¼ teaspoon ground pepper

Directions:

1. Cook frozen vegetables in the microwave according to package directions. Drain excess liquid and place the vegetables in a large bowl. Add rice, chickpeas, oil, salt and pepper; toss to combine.

Nutritional Value (Amount per Serving):

Calories: 119; Fat: 10.23; Carb: 6.76; Protein: 1.19

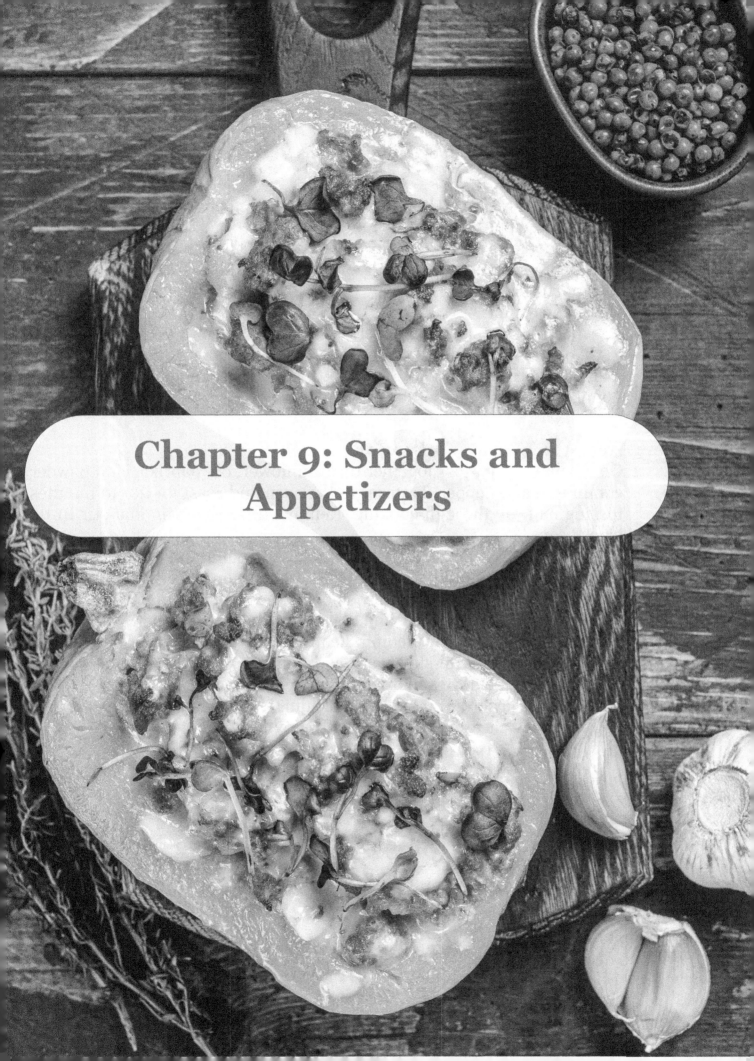

Chapter 9: Snacks and Appetizers

Roasted Cauliflower Fried Halloumi Tacos with Spicy Avocado Basil Guacamole

Prep Time: 15 Mins   Cook Time: 20 Mins   Serves: 4

Ingredients:

- 1 large, or 2 small, heads cauliflower, cut into florets
- 2 tablespoons sesame or olive oil
- 2 teaspoons smoked paprika
- 1 teaspoon chili powder
- 1 teaspoon cumin
- 1 teaspoon kosher salt and pepper
- 1 (14 ounce) can black beans, drained and rinsed
- 8 ounces halloumi cheese, sliced
- 1 cucumber or zucchini, shredded
- picy Avocado Basil Guacamole
- 1 avocado, halved
- 1 cup fresh basil
- 1/4 cup toasted pine nuts
- 1 jalapeno
- juice of 1 lemon
- 2 tablespoons sesame oil
- kosher salt and pepper

Directions:

1. Preheat the oven to 400 degrees F.
2. On a baking sheet, toss together the cauliflower, oil, paprika, chili powder, cumin, salt and pepper. Transfer to the oven and roast for 20-30 minutes, tossing halfway through cooking. Remove from the oven and stir in the black beans.
3. Meanwhile, make the avocado guacamole. Add half the avocado, basil, pine nuts, jalapeño (remove seeds for less heat), lemon juice and oil to a food processor and pulse until chunky smooth. Dice the remaining avocado half and stir into the pesto. Taste and season with salt and pepper.
4. Heat a small skillet over medium heat and add a drizzle of olive oil. Once hot, add the Halloumi slices and cook for 1-2 minutes per side or until lightly golden. Remove and drain onto paper towels.
5. To assemble, layer the cucumber, zucchini, and cauliflower in the tortillas. Top with fried cheese and guacamole. Enjoy!!

Nutritional Value (Amount per Serving):

Calories: 562; Fat: 47.15; Carb: 27.13; Protein: 16.77

Roasted Stuffed Delicata Squash

Prep Time: 15 Mins   Cook Time: 30 Mins   Serves: 4

Ingredients:

- or The Squash
- 2 delicata squash that are similar in size

- Extra virgin olive oil
- Kosher salt
- 1 teaspoon ground cinnamon divided
- ½ teaspoon ground nutmeg
- or The Filling Mixture
- 1 cup farro
- Kosher salt
- 1 shallot chopped
- 2 green onions white and green parts, trimmed and chopped
- 2 garlic cloves minced
- ⅓to ½ cup walnuts
- ⅓to ½ cup hazelnuts
- ⅓cup dried fruit such as cranberries or raisins

Directions:

1. Heat the oven to 425 degrees F and position a rack in the middle.
2. Wash the delicata squash and dry well. To make it easier to slice, place them (whole) in the microwave and warm for 2 to 3 minutes. Carefully remove them from the oven and slice each in half length-wise (use an oven mitten or wait until the squash is cool enough to handle). Using a spoon, scoop out the seeds making a cavity for the filling (discard the seeds or you can clean and roast them for later use).
3. Brush the flesh, cleaned side of the delicata squash with olive oil (including the cavity). Season with kosher salt. Mix the ground cinnamon and nutmeg in a small bowl, and season the delicata squash with ½ of this mixture.
4. On a large baking sheet, arrange the delicata squash halves, flesh-side down.
5. Roast in the heated oven for 25 minutes or until fully cooked and tender. Using a pair of tongs, flip the squash over and return to the oven for just 5 more minutes.
6. While the squash is roasting, prepare the filling. First, cook the farro in boiling salted water according to package instructions (mine took 2 cups of boiling water and 20 minutes of cooking time. Farro should absorb the cooking liquid. It is ready when it is tender and somewhat chewy).
7. In a large skillet heat 2 tablespoons extra virgin olive oil, cook the shallots, onions and garlic over medium heat, tossing for a bit, until softened (3 to 5 minutes). Season with kosher salt and the remaining nutmeg and cinnamon. Add in the nuts and dried fruit, and cook until warmed through. Add the cooked farro and toss to combine.
8. Assemble the stuffed squash. When the squash is ready, transfer the squash halves to a serving platter. Spoon the farro filling into each squash cavity. Serve!

Nutritional Value (Amount per Serving):

Calories: 272; Fat: 17.16; Carb: 27.73; Protein: 6.2

Sun-Dried Tomato Hummus And Roasted Broccoli Crostini

Prep Time: 10 Mins   Cook Time: 15 Mins   Serves: 6 To 12

Ingredients:

- oasted Broccoli
- 1 large bunch broccoli, sliced into bite-sized florets
- 2 tablespoons extra-virgin olive oil
- Salt and freshly ground pepper, to taste
- rostini
- 1 loaf of crusty whole grain bread, sliced
- Olive oil, for brushing
- Lemon wedges and red pepper flakes, for garnish
- un-Dried Tomato Hummus
- 1/4 cup tahini
- 1/4 cup fresh lemon juice (about 1 large lemon, juiced)
- 2 tablespoons olive oil, plus more for serving
- 3/4 cup drained oil-packed sun-dried tomatoes (I used one 6.7-ounce jar, drained)
- 1 large garlic clove, roughly chopped
- 1/2 teaspoon salt, more to taste
- 1/8 teaspoon red pepper flakes
- One (15-ounce) can of chickpeas, also called garbanzo beans, drained and rinsed
- 2 to 3 tablespoons water, optional

Directions:

1. To roast the broccoli: Preheat oven to 425 degrees Fahrenheit with a rack in the middle of the oven and another rack in the upper third. On a large, rimmed baking sheet, toss broccoli florets with 2 tablespoons olive oil and a sprinkling of salt and pepper. Roast for 15 to 20 minutes on the middle rack, tossing halfway, until the edges are turning golden and crispy.
2. To toast the bread: Brush both sides of your sliced bread lightly with olive oil and place them on a separate baking sheet. Bake for 6 to 10 minutes on the top rack (larger slices will require more baking time), turning halfway, until lightly golden and toasted. Remove from oven and set aside.
3. To make the hummus: First, you'll whip the tahini and lemon juice together to make them ultra smooth and creamy. Combine the tahini and

lemon juice in the bowl of your food processor (a smaller food processor will be better suited to the job) or high-powered blender (i.e. Vitamix or Blendtec). Process for about 1 1/2 minutes, pausing to scrape down the bowl of your processor as necessary.

4. Add the olive oil, sun-dried tomatoes, chopped garlic, salt and red pepper flakes to the whipped tahini and lemon juice mixture. Process for about 1 minute, pausing to scrape down the bowl as necessary.

5. Add half of the chickpeas to the food processor and process for 1 minute. Scrape down the bowl, then add the remaining chickpeas and process for until the hummus is thick and quite smooth, about 1 to 2 minutes more. If your hummus is too thick or hasn't yet blended into creamy oblivion, run the food processor while drizzling in 2 to 3 tablespoons water, until it reaches your desired consistency.

6. To assemble your crostini: Top each piece of toast with a generous spread of hummus. Roughly chop the broccoli into small pieces, then top each toast with broccoli. Finish them off with a small sprinkle of lemon juice and red pepper flakes. Serve immediately.

7. Store hummus in an airtight container and refrigerate for up to one week. Crostini is best when assembled just before serving.

Nutritional Value (Amount per Serving):

Calories: 209; Fat: 13.47; Carb: 11.28; Protein: 11.59

Greek Tomato Feta Fritters (Domatokeftethes)

Prep Time: 15 Mins   Cook Time: 50 Mins   Serves: 4

Ingredients:

- 2 cups diced fresh tomatoes with juices
- ½ cup packed grated zucchini
- ⅓cup sliced green onions
- 2 teaspoons kosher salt, or to taste
- 1 teaspoon white sugar
- ½ teaspoon freshly ground black pepper
- ¼ teaspoon dried oregano
- 1 pinch cayenne pepper
- ¼ cup chopped fresh Italian parsley
- 2 tablespoons chopped fresh mint
- 2 tablespoons chopped fresh basil
- 3 ounces feta cheese, crumbled
- ¾ cup all-purpose flour, or more as needed
- ¾ teaspoon baking powder
- vegetable oil for frying

Directions:

1. Gather all ingredients.
2. Stir together tomatoes, zucchini, green onions, kosher salt, sugar, black pepper, oregano, and cayenne in a bowl to combine. Let sit for 15 minutes for the sugar and salt to draw out liquids from the vegetables.
3. Stir the tomato mixture; add parsley, mint, and basil. Crumble in feta cheese. Add flour and baking powder; mix with a spoon until combined. Batter should be relatively loose but will hold its shape on a spoon. If too loose, add more flour; if too dry, add some water until desired consistency is reached. Wrap the bowl in plastic wrap and let chill in the refrigerator for at least 30 minutes.
4. Heat 1 inch of vegetable oil in a frying pan over medium-high heat to 350 degrees F, or use a deep fryer.
5. Place heaping tablespoonfuls of batter in the hot oil; reduce heat to medium. Fry until golden brown and cooked through, 2 to 3 minutes per side.
6. Flip once more and fry for an additional 30 seconds, if desired.
7. Serve warm or at room temperature.

Nutritional Value (Amount per Serving):

Calories: 463; Fat: 23.29; Carb: 25.36; Protein: 37.14

Proper British Fish Cakes

Prep Time: 15 Mins   Cook Time: 35 Mins   Serves: 4

Ingredients:

- or The Tartar Sauce:
- ½ cup mayonnaise
- 2 tablespoons capers, drained and chopped
- 1 tablespoon finely chopped shallot
- 1 tablespoon finely chopped Italian parsley
- 1 tablespoon finely chopped fresh tarragon
- 2 teaspoons prepared horseradish
- 1 teaspoon Dijon mustard
- 1 pinch cayenne pepper
- or The Fish Cakes:
- ½ cup milk
- 1 bay leaf
- 1 pound cod, cut into 1-inch pieces
- salt and freshly ground black pepper to taste
- 12 ounces russet potato, peeled and quartered

- 1 pinch cayenne pepper
- 1 tablespoon finely chopped Italian parsley
- 1 tablespoon sliced fresh chives
- 1 teaspoon finely grated lemon zest
- or The Breading:
- ⅓cup all-purpose flour
- 1 large egg, beaten
- 1 cup panko bread crumbs, or as needed
- ¼ cup vegetable oil, or as needed

Directions:

1. Gather all ingredients.
2. Mix mayonnaise, capers, shallot, parsley, tarragon, horseradish, mustard, and cayenne together in a bowl for tartar sauce and refrigerate until needed.
3. Add milk and bay leaf to a saucepan, and place the pieces of fish over the top. Season with salt. Bring to a simmer over medium heat, and cook for about 1 minute, stirring occasionally. As soon as the fish firms up, but before it starts to flake apart, turn off the heat and cover. Let sit for 5 minutes before draining. Let cool, about 10 minutes. Refrigerate until needed.
4. Meanwhile, bring a pot of lightly salted water to a boil. Add russet potato and boil until tender but not falling apart.
5. Drain and mash potato in a bowl. Season with salt, black pepper, and cayenne. Add parsley, chives, and lemon zest; add 1 tablespoon tartar sauce mixture. Mix until combined.
6. Flake chilled fish over the top. Mix until combined.
7. Scoop out ¼ of the mixture and form into a patty. Repeat with remaining mixture.
8. Dust cakes with flour on both sides. Brush both sides of cakes with beaten egg. Coat in bread crumbs.
9. Heat oil in a skillet over medium heat. Pan-fry patties in the hot oil until golden brown and heated through, 3 to 4 minutes per side.
10. Drain on paper towels.
11. Serve with tartar sauce and enjoy!

Nutritional Value (Amount per Serving):

Calories: 702; Fat: 42.68; Carb: 33.79; Protein: 43.59

Toasted Ravioli

Prep Time: 10 Mins   Cook Time: 15 Mins   Serves: 3-4

Ingredients:

- 1/2 pound ravioli (any flavor), fresh or thawed from frozen

- 1/3 cup all-purpose flour
- 1/2 teaspoon garlic powder
- 1/2 teaspoon paprika
- 1/2 teaspoon Italian seasoning
- 1/2 teaspoon salt
- 1/4 teaspoon black pepper
- 2 large eggs, beaten
- 1 cup Panko breadcrumbs
- vegetable oil (for frying), about 3 cups
- 1/4 cup Parmesan cheese, freshly grated (optional, for serving)
- 2 tablespoons fresh parsley, chopped (optional, for serving)
- 1/2 cup marinara sauce (for serving)

Directions:

1. In a large mixing bowl (or ziploc bag), add ravioli, flour, garlic powder, paprika, Italian seasoning, salt, and pepper. Mix well until evenly coated.
2. Prepare 2 separate shallow bowls and place the beaten eggs in one and the breadcrumbs in the other. Dip the ravioli, one piece at a time, in the egg and then coat it with the breadcrumbs. You can gently press the crumbs into the ravioli to adhere as much as possible.
3. In a medium cooking pot, add enough oil to fill the pot at least 2 inches deep. Preheat the oil over medium-high heat for 3-4 minutes until the hot oil shimmers.
4. Deep fry the breaded ravioli in batches (about 4-5 pieces each time) until golden brown, about 1-2 minutes. Turn the ravioli occasionally to get an even golden crust on all sides.
5. Transfer the ravioli onto a paper towel lined plate to drain any excess oil and allow them to cool for 5 minutes before serving.
6. Transfer to a serving plate and sprinkle with Parmesan cheese and fresh parsley. Serve warm with marinara sauce.

Nutritional Value (Amount per Serving):

Calories: 273; Fat: 16.64; Carb: 23.97; Protein: 7.5

Chapter 10: Desserts

Oreo Fluff Salad

Prep Time: 15 Mins   Cook Time: 1 Hr   Serves: 12

Ingredients:

- 4 cups milk
- 2 (3.4 ounce) packages instant vanilla pudding mix
- (8 ounce) containers whipped topping
- 30 chocolate sandwich cookies, crushed, or to taste

Directions:

1. Whisk together milk and instant pudding mix in a large serving bowl until thickened, about 2 minutes. Fold in whipped topping until incorporated.
2. Stir crushed cookies into pudding until well blended. Cover the bowl with plastic wrap. Refrigerate until chilled and thickened, at least 1 hour to overnight.

Nutritional Value (Amount per Serving):

Calories: 252; Fat: 8.52; Carb: 40.6; Protein: 4.14

Easter Meat Pie

Prep Time: 45 Mins   Cook Time: 1 Hr   Serves: 12

Ingredients:

- 2 pounds ricotta cheese
- 6 large eggs
- 1 pound cooked ham, chopped
- ½ pound Genoa salami, chopped
- ½ pound mozzarella cheese, grated
- ¼ pound prosciutto, chopped
- 4(9 inch) unbaked pie crusts
- ¼ cup grated Parmesan cheese

Directions:

1. Preheat the oven to 325 degrees F.
2. Place ricotta in a large mixing bowl. Beat in eggs, one at a time, with an electric mixer on low speed. Stir in ham, salami, mozzarella, and prosciutto until well combined.
3. Line two 9-inch pans with pastry. Divide ricotta mixture between the pans. Sprinkle each pie with Parmesan cheese, then cover with top pastry. Crimp the edges and cut steam vents in tops.
4. Bake in the preheated oven until crust is golden brown, about 1 hour. Cool pies on wire racks.

Nutritional Value (Amount per Serving):

Calories: 591; Fat: 37.17; Carb: 30.94; Protein: 32.81

Creamy Rice Pudding

Prep Time: 10 Mins   Cook Time: 40 Mins   Serves: 4

Ingredients:

- 1 ½ cups cold water
- ¾ cup uncooked white rice
- 2 cups milk, divided
- ⅓ cup white sugar
- ¼ teaspoon salt
- 1 egg, beaten
- ⅔ cup golden raisins
- 1 tablespoon butter
- ½ teaspoon vanilla extract

Directions:

1. Pour water into a saucepan and bring to a boil over medium heat; stir in rice. Reduce heat to low, cover, and simmer until rice is tender and liquid has been absorbed, about 20 minutes.
2. Combine cooked rice, 1 1/2 cups milk, sugar, and salt in a clean saucepan. Cook over medium heat, stirring often, until thick and creamy, about 15 minutes.
3. Stir in remaining 1/2 cup milk, beaten egg, and raisins; cook 2 more minutes, stirring constantly. Remove from heat and stir in butter and vanilla until combined; serve warm.

Nutritional Value (Amount per Serving):

Calories: 383; Fat: 12.78; Carb: 58.56; Protein: 9.89

Easy Baklava

Prep Time: 30 Mins   Cook Time: 50 Mins   Serves: 36

Ingredients:

- 1 pound chopped nuts
- 1 teaspoon ground cinnamon
- 1 (16 ounce) package phyllo dough
- 1 cup butter, melted
- 1 cup white sugar
- 1 cup water
- ½ cup honey
- 1 teaspoon vanilla extract
- 1 teaspoon grated lemon zest

Directions:

1. Preheat the oven to 350 degrees F. Butter a 9x13-inch baking dish.
2. Toss together nuts and cinnamon. Unroll phyllo and cut the whole stack in half to fit the dish. Cover phyllo with a damp cloth while assembling the baklava, to keep it from drying out.
3. Place 2 sheets of phyllo in the bottom of the prepared dish. Brush generously with some of the melted butter. Sprinkle 2 to 3 tablespoons of the nut mixture on top. Repeat layers until all ingredients are used, ending

with about 6 sheets of phyllo.

4. Using a sharp knife, cut baklava into 4 long rows, then diagonally 9 times to make 36 diamond shapes. Be sure to cut all the way through to the bottom of the layers.

5. Bake in the preheated oven until golden brown and crisp, about 50 minutes.

6. While baklava is baking, combine sugar and water in a small saucepan over medium heat and bring to a boil. Stir in honey, vanilla, and lemon zest; reduce heat and simmer 20 minutes.

7. Remove baklava from the oven and immediately spoon syrup over it. Let cool completely before serving. Store uncovered.

Nutritional Value (Amount per Serving):

Calories: 159; Fat: 14.83; Carb: 6.59; Protein: 1.99

Rose Water Rice Pudding

Prep Time: 10 Mins   Cook Time: 45 Mins   Serves: 14

Ingredients:

- 4 cups water
- 2 cups uncooked long grain rice
- 4 cups half-and-half cream
- 1-1/2 cups sugar
- 1 to 2 teaspoons rose water
- Optional: Pomegranate seeds and chopped pistachios

Directions:

1. In a heavy saucepan, combine water and rice; bring to a boil over medium heat. Reduce heat; cover and simmer until water is absorbed, about 15 minutes. Add cream and sugar; bring to a boil. Reduce heat; simmer, uncovered, until slightly thickened, 30-40 minutes. Stir in rose water. Refrigerate until chilled, at least 2 hours. Stir in additional cream to reach desired consistency. If desired, top with pomegranate seeds and pistachios.

Nutritional Value (Amount per Serving):

Calories: 174; Fat: 1.94; Carb: 35.49; Protein: 4.16

One-Bowl Yogurt And Honey Olive Oil Cake

Prep Time: 15 Mins   Cook Time: 45 Mins   Serves: 8 To 12

Ingredients:

- 1 cup whole or 2% plain Greek yogurt

- 2/3 cup olive oil, plus more for coating the pan
- 2/3 cup honey
- 1 tablespoon finely chopped fresh thyme leaves
- 1 teaspoon finely grated lemon zest
- 3 large eggs
- 1 1/2 cups all-purpose flour
- 1/2 teaspoon baking powder
- 1/2 teaspoon baking soda
- 1/4 teaspoon salt

Directions:

1. Arrange a rack in the middle of the oven and heat to 325°F.
2. Grease a 9-inch round cake pan or springform pan lightly with oil. Line the bottom with parchment paper and grease the paper if using a cake pan.
3. Whisk together the yogurt, olive oil, honey, thyme, and lemon zest in a large bowl. Add the eggs, one at a time, whisking well after each addition. Add the flour, baking powder, baking soda, and salt. Stir with a rubber spatula until the batter is almost smooth with just a few small lumps, but do not overmix.
4. Transfer the batter to the cake pan, and use a spatula to spread it out evenly. Bake until the top is lightly browned and a tester comes out clean, 40 to 45 minutes.
5. Transfer the cake to a cooling rack and let it cool for 10 minutes before removing it from the pan. Run a knife around the pan to loosen. If using a springform pan, unclasp the sides. Otherwise, flip the cake onto a plate and flip it back onto the rack or serving plate. Serve warm or at room temperature.

Nutritional Value (Amount per Serving):

Calories: 316; Fat: 18.33; Carb: 35.26; Protein: 4.09

Cinnamon Palmiers

Prep Time: 30 Mins   Cook Time: 20 Mins   Serves: 24

Ingredients:

- ⅓ cup white sugar
- ¾ teaspoon ground cinnamon
- ⅛ teaspoon ground cardamom
- ¼ cup white sugar
- 1 sheet frozen puff pastry, thawed
- 1 tablespoon butter, melted

Directions:

1. Gather all ingredients.
2. Mix 1/3 cup sugar, cinnamon, and cardamom together in a small bowl.
3. Sprinkle remaining 1/4 cup sugar onto a work surface. Unfold puff pastry

and place over sugar; roll out to a 10x15-inch rectangle. Brush pastry with melted butter, then sprinkle sugar mixture evenly over top.

4. Starting with one long edge, roll pastry tightly around filling, stopping in the middle of the rectangle.
5. Repeat with the opposite edge, rolling to the center and meeting the first roll. Wet your finger with water and dot along the long edges where the two rolls touch; press gently to seal. Refrigerate until slightly firm, 5 to 10 minutes.
6. Meanwhile, preheat the oven to 375 degrees F. Line a baking sheet with parchment paper.
7. Cut chilled pastry into 1/4-inch slices; place 1 inch apart onto the prepared baking sheet.
8. Bake in the preheated oven until golden and crisp, about 12 minutes. Let rest briefly on the baking sheet before transferring to a wire rack to cool completely.

Nutritional Value (Amount per Serving):

Calories: 26; Fat: 2.16; Carb: 1.57; Protein: 0.29

Authentic Italian Rice Pudding

Prep Time: 10 Mins   Cook Time: 2 Hrs 50 Mins   Serves: 8

Ingredients:

- 6 cups whole milk
- ¾ cup Arborio rice
- ¾ cup white sugar, divided
- 1 teaspoon vanilla extract
- ¼ teaspoon salt
- 2 eggs
- 2 egg yolks
- 1 cup heavy whipping cream

Directions:

1. Mix milk, rice, 1/2 of the sugar, vanilla extract, and salt together in a saucepan over medium-high heat. Bring to a boil.
2. Blend remaining sugar with whole eggs and yolks in a bowl to make a creamy custard.
3. Reduce heat of the milk mixture. Let simmer, uncovered, until thickened, 30 to 40 minutes. Fold in the custard. Heat until thickened again, about 5 more minutes.
4. Beat cream in a chilled glass or metal bowl with an electric mixer until soft peaks form.
5. Remove the milk and custard mixture from heat. Let cool, about 10 minutes. Fold in the whipped cream. Pour pudding into a serving dish, cover, and refrigerate until chilled, at least 2 hours.

Nutritional Value (Amount per Serving):

Calories: 341; Fat: 20.63; Carb: 32.37; Protein: 10.68

Spanakopita Recipe (Greek Spinach Pie)

Prep Time: 20 Mins   Cook Time: 1 Hr   Serves: 12

Ingredients:

- or The Spinach And Feta Filling
- 16 oz frozen chopped spinach, thawed and well-drained
- 2 bunches flat-leaf parsley, stems trimmed, finely chopped
- 1 large yellow onion, finely chopped
- 2 garlic cloves, minced
- 2 tbsp Private Reserve extra virgin olive oil
- 4 eggs
- 10.5 oz quality feta cheese, crumbled
- 2 tsp dried dill weed
- Freshly-ground black pepper
- or The Crust
- 1 16 oz package The Fillo Factory Organic Dough (#4 pastry sheets), properly thawed (see tips above)
- 1 cup Private Reserve extra virgin olive oil, more if needed

Directions:

1. Preheat the oven to 325 degrees F.
2. Before you begin mixing the filling, be sure the spinach is very well drained, and squeeze out any excess liquid by hand.
3. To make the filling: In a mixing bowl, add the spinach and the remaining filling ingredients. Stir until all is well-combined.
4. Unroll the phyllo (fillo) sheets and place them between two slightly damp kitchen cloths.
5. Prepare a 9 1/2 X 13 baking dish like this one. Brush the bottom and sides of the dish with olive oil.
6. To assemble the spanakopita: Line the baking dish with two sheets of phyllo (fillo) letting them cover the sides of the dish. Brush with olive oil. Add two more sheets in the same manner, and brush them with olive oil. Repeat until two-thirds of the phyllo (fillo) is used up.
7. Now, evenly spread the spinach and feta filling over the phyllo (fillo) crust. Top with two more sheets, and brush with olive oil.
8. Continue to layer the phyllo (fillo) sheets, two-at-a-time, brushing with olive oil, until you have used up all the sheets. Brush the very top layer with olive oil, and sprinkle with just a few drops of water.
9. Fold the flaps or excess from the sides, you can crumble them a little. Brush the folded sides well with olive oil. Cut Spanakopita ONLY PART-WAY through into squares, or leave the cutting to later.
10. Bake in the 325 degrees F heated-oven for 1 hour, or until the phyllo (fillo)

crust is crisp and golden brown. Remove from the oven. Finish cutting into squares and serve. Enjoy!

Nutritional Value (Amount per Serving):

Calories: 434; Fat: 30.72; Carb: 22.46; Protein: 17.17

Crispy Sesame Feta Fingers with Honey

Prep Time: 10 Mins   Cook Time: 8 Mins   Serves: 4

Ingredients:

- 1 (8 ounce) slice feta cheese
- ½ cup all-purpose flour
- 1 egg, beaten
- ½ cup sesame seeds
- 1 pinch ground black pepper to taste
- ¼ cup olive oil
- 2 tablespoons honey, or more to taste

Directions:

1. Slice feta into four fingers and place in the freezer for 10 minutes to help the cheese hold its shape while you prepare the other ingredients.
2. Set out egg, flour, and sesame seeds in three separate shallow dishes. Season egg with black pepper.
3. Pour oil into a small skillet to a depth of about 1/2-inch. Heat over medium-high heat.
4. Remove feta from freezer and dredge each finger first in egg, then flour, egg again, followed by sesame seeds. Evenly coat all sides. Add breaded fingers to the hot oil.
5. Cook until golden brown, about 2 minutes per side. Remove from oil and briefly drain excess oil on kitchen towel.
6. Place feta fingers on a serving plate and drizzle with honey. Enjoy immediately while hot.

Nutritional Value (Amount per Serving):

Calories: 388; Fat: 29.37; Carb: 24.83; Protein: 9.34

APPENDIX RECIPE INDEX

Made in the USA
Las Vegas, NV
06 March 2024

86819762R00063